Building on
Emergent
Curriculum

The Power of Play for School Readiness

Sarah Taylor Vanover, EdD

Gryphon House

www.gryphonhouse.com

Copyright

Published by Gryphon House, Inc.
P. O. Box 10, Lewisville, NC 27023
800.638.0928; 877.638.7576 [fax]

Visit us on the web at www.gryphonhouse.com.

Library of Congress Cataloging-in-Publication Data

The cataloging-in-publication data is registered with the Library of Congress for ISBN 978-0-87659-845-0.

Bulk Purchase

Gryphon House books are available for special premiums and sales promotions as well as for fund-raising use. Special editions or book excerpts also can be created to specifications. For details, call 800.638.0928.

Disclaimer

Gryphon House, Inc., cannot be held responsible for damage, mishap, or injury incurred during the use of or because of activities in this book. Appropriate and reasonable caution and adult supervision of children involved in activities and corresponding to the age and capability of each child involved are recommended at all times. Do not leave children unattended at any time. Observe safety and caution at all times.

Dedication

This book is dedicated to my good friend, Jessica, who is truly devoted to emergent curriculum in the preschool classroom!

Table of Contents

Introduction

Story 1: Megan's Emergent-Curriculum Lesson

Several years ago, while observing Head Start classrooms as a curriculum coach, I had the opportunity to observe a teacher whom I will call Megan. On that day, Megan and her assistant teacher had a well-developed lesson plan focused on living and nonliving things. In the math center, Megan had created sorting activities in which children could categorize small plastic models of animals, plants, and household objects. The sand table contained pretend fossils that the children could dig up, and Megan's assistant teacher sat at the art table to help children with a collage activity that involved cutting out pictures of living and nonliving things from magazines.

During the observation, I noticed that three boys in the block area—whom I will call Santiago, Jamir, and Hassan—were getting louder and louder. While I could not see exactly what was happening, I noticed that they were using some of the longest wooden blocks (about two feet each) and that small matchbox cars were zooming out of their center into the workspaces of other children.

Unlike what many early childhood educators would have done, Megan did not speak to the boys right away. Instead, she stood back and observed them for a few minutes. Then, as the boys talked about how fast their cars were, Megan sat down beside them and asked, "Who has the fastest car?" When I took a closer look, I saw that the boys had been using the long blocks as racetracks for their cars.

Megan asked if she could watch the next race. The boys obliged, lining up their blocks, counting down, and pushing their cars toward the finish line. When Hassan announced that he had won, Megan began asking all three boys questions that encouraged them to think critically, such as "What's different about Hassan's car?" and "Why do you think he won?" She then had Santiago use some smaller blocks to prop up the starting end of his long block. Santiago won the next race, and the boys began to create theories about why. Then Megan asked Jamir to prop up the starting end of his long block even higher than Santiago had. This time, Jamir won.

By this time, the boys began to realize that something about the positions of the blocks was affecting how fast their cars raced. Megan asked the three of them to predict what would happen if they propped up a long block with more or fewer small blocks. Once they did, Megan introduced the term *inclined plane* to let the boys know that what they were doing had a scientific name.

As the boys repeated their races, they began to ask Megan which car was winning the most. Megan brought over a large piece of chart paper and some red, green, and blue markers. She asked the boys how they could use these tools to show which car was winning the most races. The boys began drawing a blue car on the paper every time the blue car won. At this point, Megan stepped away from the block area and began to interact with the other children in the classroom.

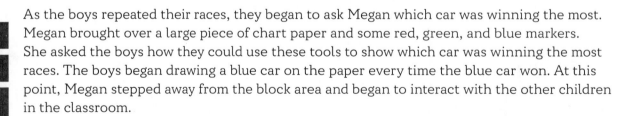

Santiago, Jamir, and Hassan stayed in the block area until free play ended twenty-five minutes later. They did not complete the collage project with the teaching assistant, and no one wanted to ruin the chart by dividing it up among the boys, so they had no physical products to take home to their families. However, when Jamir's grandmother arrived to pick him up and asked him whether he had made anything that day, Jamir responded, "I made an entwined [sic] plane. Did you know that entwined planes make you faster?"

Story 2: Nicole's Theme-Based Lesson

Later that week, I went to observe another Head Start classroom. The teacher, whom I will call Nicole, had received high praise from family members and coworkers because of her dedication to her students and the hours she spent working on her classroom and lessons. I was excited to see her in action.

I entered the classroom before the children arrived, and I immediately noticed an explosion of colors and hanging objects. Some were children's artwork, and some were adult-made posters with encouragements such as "Smile at your friend today!" or "Gentle hands make a peaceful day!" Each learning center also had a detailed project or intricate objects that corresponded with trees, the current curricular theme:

- **Art area:** paper, glue sticks, and many different cut-out pieces (brown trunks, green leaves, yellow suns, and so on) for the children to assemble and glue onto the papers to show the life cycle of a tree. A finished example was displayed toward the back of the table.
- **Sensory table:** acorns, twigs, and leaves for the children to make their own trees
- **Science area:** potting soil, seeds, construction paper, and glue for the children to create pictures of planting. A finished example was displayed here, too.
- **Dramatic-play center:** a sculpted papier-mâché tree attached to the wall and artificial leaves hanging from the ceiling, creating a "forest" to play in

During morning drop-off time, Nicole greeted families while the children put away their backpacks and went straight to the gathering rug, where they waited patiently for her. Clearly there was a well-established routine in the classroom. When Nicole arrived on the rug, she sang two or three songs with the children and then read them a book about how Timmy the Tree changed during each season. Then Nicole explained the day's activity for each of the classroom centers, assigned each child to a center, and set the timer for fifteen minutes. Her assistant teacher, whom I will call Yasmine, went to the art table to help the children with the life-cycle pictures, and Nicole went to the science area to assist the children with gluing the dirt and seeds.

I could tell that the children were enamored with Nicole. When she sat down in the science center, the four children there crowded around her and tried to sit as close to her as possible. She began to tell them how to complete the science activity. One child reached into the bag of potting soil, and Nicole immediately redirected him to place his hands in his lap. Later, when another child did not pick up her bottle of glue as instructed, Nicole used hand-over-hand assistance to help her spread the glue on her paper. After explaining one step of the project, Nicole waited for all four children to complete the directions before moving on to the next step, meaning that some children had to wait several minutes to proceed. Another child left the table and took some magnifying glasses off the science shelves, but Nicole stood up and helped him put the magnifying glasses down and return to the table.

Similar things happened in the art center. Yasmine passed out the various cut-out pieces to each child and let them practice arranging the pieces on sheets of paper. If a child could not duplicate the arrangement on the sample, Yasmine used hand-over-hand assistance to help the child place the pieces. Once all the children had arranged the pieces correctly, Yasmine gave each child a glue stick and told them all to secure the pieces to their papers. The children sat at the table until all the papers were complete.

Once the timer went off, the children rotated to new stations, and the same processes began again. Between Nicole and Yasmine, each child heard at least two discussions about the life cycles of trees, and each child had at least two papers to take home at the end of the day. But how much learning had these students done, really?

Why the Difference?

Nicole's classroom was somewhat (and unintentionally) deceiving to staff and families for several reasons:

- Everyone could see the amount of work that Nicole dedicated to setting up the classroom environment.
- The theme was well established throughout the classroom.
- The children frequently brought papers and projects home as evidence of their learning.

What the families did not understand was that Nicole's teaching style did not really prepare her students for kindergarten. They were learning to follow a schedule and follow directions, which are important skills for elementary school. But the classroom format did not allow them to practice other crucial school skills, such as cutting, gluing, having back-and-forth conversations with one another, and creatively solving problems.

Furthermore, the children in Nicole's classroom did not get to explore or develop their own creativity. Each center had only one activity, and the children had no choice but to participate in it. The theme of trees did not seem to capture their interest, but when they attempted to look at unrelated materials or use supplies in a different way than intended, the teachers verbally or physically redirected them. To make matters worse, the assignments did not challenge the children. They simply copied what the teachers had already completed.

Megan, the other teacher I observed, had also created a detailed lesson plan and set up complementary activities. However, she let her students use the classroom materials freely, and she took the time to see what caught their interest and then to change her plans based

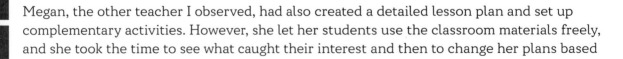

on their needs. In other words, her classroom used an *emergent curriculum*. Megan's impromptu lesson with Santiago, Jamir, and Hassan incorporated problem solving, advanced language, peer interaction, and components of the scientific method (creating and testing a hypothesis and documenting the results). Not only had she guided the boys with complex questions, but she had also stepped back when appropriate and let them figure out what to do. Because Santiago, Jamir, and Hassan were interested in this activity, they enjoyed their experience and were more likely to learn than if Megan had forced them to participate in a theme-based activity. At the end of the day, while the boys had no physical evidence of their learning, they had learned new concepts that they could apply to many future lessons.

After observing both classrooms, I could clearly tell that Megan's students showed higher levels of learning than Nicole's students. However, I began to wonder how the families viewed each classroom. Megan and Nicole both gave time and effort to their students, but Megan focused on the children's interests instead of on her own ideas of what the curriculum should include. That is the core principle of emergent curriculum: to follow the children's interests to make the curriculum more engaging and motivate students to learn more deeply. Teachers and families alike need to understand that deep learning does not always result in concrete products. Deep learning happens through conversations, introduction of new vocabulary, hands-on explorations, and experiments.

Purposes of This Book

My goal is to show you how to teach as Megan did. In this book, we will learn how to use emergent curriculum to create project-based activities that use play as the primary classroom learning tool. We will find out how both teachers and students benefit from following the children's interests when creating lesson plans and setting up classroom environments. We will discover how to observe, learn about, and plan according to students' interests and abilities instead of merely reusing the same lesson plans and materials every school year.

Furthermore, this book will show us how children can experience deep learning in the classroom without creating physical products. We will explore new ways to document children's learning and how to help families develop new expectations for that learning. When adults make these changes, preschoolers can experience deep learning that will help them develop into curious, motivated, and articulate thinkers who are ready for kindergarten.

chapter 1

Theme-Based Units in the Preschool Classroom

If the title of this book is *Building on Emergent Curriculum*, then why start with a chapter on theme-based units? As an analogy, imagine going to an unfamiliar city to visit a friend. Your GPS stops working when you are still twenty minutes from your friend's home, so you call her for directions. Her first question will probably be, "Where are you now?" You both need an accurate understanding of your starting point so your friend can guide you to your destination.

On our journey to learn about emergent curriculum, theme-based units are our starting point. They are one of the most popular methods for creating preschool lesson plans, so you probably have used them at some point in your career and perhaps still use them. This chapter examines what theme-based units are, why so many teachers use them, and why they fall short as a method of teaching young children.

What Is a Theme-Based Unit?

To create a theme-based unit, a teacher selects a topic to focus on for one or two weeks, depending on how broad it is, and plans all classroom activities for that period around that theme. Years ago, the theme may have been something whimsical, such as the circus, but today's preschool classrooms often use science or social-studies themes, such as neighborhoods, community helpers, or life cycles. Then the teacher looks at each content area on her lesson plan (such as art, dramatic play, fine motor skills, literacy, music, and math) and chooses activities for each area that link to the chosen theme. If the theme is, for example, community helpers, the lesson plan may indicate that all music selections for the week will focus on firefighters, bus drivers, and postal workers. The teacher might add dress-up clothes for doctors, grocery-store workers, and park rangers to the dramatic-play area. She might place books about cooks, teachers, and hairdressers in the classroom library. And so it goes for the remaining areas of the classroom.

Unpacking the Popularity of Theme-Based Units

Why do we commonly take a thematic approach to teaching young children? One major reason is that themes simplify lesson planning. Given an almost infinite number of possible activities to engage in with the children in her care, a teacher can more easily choose among them if she knows that they all must relate to, for example, the seasons. Beyond this key factor, several intertwined trends and concerns have contributed to the popularity of theme-based units.

The Rise of Academic Concerns in Preschool

The history of preschool in the United States really began in 1965, when the federal government first implemented the Head Start program for children living in poverty. Because only a small number of students qualified for Head Start's services, individual states began to implement their own programs to serve other low-income students. During the 1980s, as the Women's Bureau of the US Department of Labor notes, the percentage of women of all socioeconomic classes who worked outside the home rose year by year. As a result, child-care centers became more prevalent throughout the United States. The vast majority of these programs focused on keeping children healthy and safe while introducing social and emotional skills that the children would need in kindergarten. Preliteracy and prenumeracy skills did not become a focus of child-care programs until over a decade later.

From 1998 to 2010, the University of Virginia conducted a study with the US Department of Education to look at the work demands placed on kindergarten students. Researchers Daphna Bassok, Scott Latham, and Anna Rorem explain that over this twelve-year period, academic content in kindergarten—such as holding a pencil, writing one's first name, reading simple words, identifying numbers, and doing basic addition—continued to increase. This increase occurred because during the same period, standardized testing became increasingly important in elementary school. Motivated by rewards for high scores on these tests, schools began teaching academic skills earlier so that students would have more time to practice them before having to take standardized tests and therefore could score higher. Meanwhile, kindergarten students began using workbooks more frequently, and fewer play centers were established in kindergarten classrooms than in previous years.

As the demands of kindergarten increased, preschools responded. In their efforts to prepare children for kindergarten, preschool teachers began to focus on group activities in which every student did the same thing. Because teachers had so many skills to teach and so many children to teach them to, this format made it easier to make sure that every child heard the same information, regardless of individual developmental abilities. For example, though most preschool teachers did not use worksheets, many teachers began asking students to complete "art" projects in which each student arranged the same preproduced parts using the same methods to create nearly identical works.

At the same time, families became more interested in kindergarten preparation. They began wanting their children to learn more about academic content, such as handwriting and prereading skills, than about group play and taking turns. Furthermore, many family members began using full-time child care during this period and spent most of each workday away from their children. Understandably, these family members wanted to see what their children did all day. These trends led families not only to want but also to expect their children to bring home handouts and art projects, which families could use to gauge children's academic success.

Past Teacher Training

In the 1990s, when many of today's veteran preschool teachers received their training, large-group or circle time was considered the primary tool for educating young children. Therefore, teachers learned to do most of their teaching by using storybooks, dances, songs, and fingerplays focusing on a selected theme. This way, at least in theory, all the children would learn the desired content no matter what specific activity they were doing. Art projects in particular had to focus on the theme, perhaps because most children participated in daily art activities or because the finished products went home to families and helped show what the children were learning about at school.

Teacher, Administrator, and Family Expectations

Teachers' own expectations can lead them toward the use of theme-based units. For one thing, they may have experienced theme-based units in their own early childhoods. Additionally, at least in the United States, popular culture tends to portray preschool teachers as happy adults who work in brightly colored classrooms and enjoy music and art. Movies, TV shows, and books frequently depict these teachers creating beautiful bulletin boards, giving children lots of hugs, and sending home colorful handprint turkeys at Thanksgiving. Furthermore, these portrayals typically show classrooms using teacher-created, theme-based units. Such pervasive media messages can strongly influence teachers, even when they desire to do things differently.

Administrators also contribute to the use of theme-based units. For instance, a given child-care program may use an established theme-based curriculum that the teachers must follow. This curriculum may be used to recruit families and provide diverse topics for teachers to discuss with children throughout the preschool or calendar year. This way of doing things may reassure both administrators and families that the children learn about a wide variety of content areas and therefore become more prepared for kindergarten.

Family expectations also contribute to theme-based units in another way. When families pay for full-time child care, they may want concrete evidence of what that money goes toward each day. Thus, families and administrators may ask teachers to choose activities that result in papers and artwork that children can take home. Teachers can easily plan these kinds of projects when using theme-based units. Unfortunately, some important content that early childhood professionals teach—such as problem solving or math and science concepts—does not typically lend itself to making physical products.

The DIY Generation of Teachers

Because theme-based units have been the standard for so long in preschool education, we can find many curriculum books full of preplanned two-week lessons that include thematic activities for every learning center in the classroom. These books appeal to busy educators, particularly those who feel burned out or who lack experience in lesson planning. And with these resources available, who can blame these teachers for not wanting to reinvent the wheel, as it were?

These books feed into the popular do-it-yourself (DIY) movement, with intriguing implications for teaching. In many DIY endeavors, someone creates step-by-step instructions to show how simple a project—anything from home improvement to cake decorating to arts and crafts to gardening—can be. Once these instructions launch on the internet, commonly as a video or as a post on a community bulletin-board site, anyone can recreate that project at home.

The DIY movement has given millions of men and women the confidence to take on previously intimidating projects—including teaching. Combining DIY resources and theme-based units makes lesson planning go quickly. A teacher can simply open a bulletin-board site and search for, say, "easy preschool nature activities" and instantly find all the ideas and projects she could ever want, complete with instructions and pictures of finished samples. She simply has to decide which activities to use on which days.

The Pitfalls of Theme-Based Units

While theme-based units are traditional and popular, they are not the best way to teach young children. Let's explore some of the reasons why.

Lack of True Creative Expression

 Case Study: "Creative" Dinosaur Art

Vaani wants to arrange some art projects for her class's unit on dinosaurs. She searches a bulletin-board site and finds an activity that involves gluing cut-out shapes onto a sheet of paper to create a dinosaur. Vaani cuts out many identical shapes so that each child can have a full set. Then she glues one dinosaur together and mounts it by the art table. At learning-center time the next day, as Vaani gives the directions for the art center, she says, "It's your turn to make dinosaurs, just like that one," and points to her creation.

The problem with this DIY-style art activity is that creative expression is actually removed from the equation. DIY projects, contrary to popular belief, do not really create anything new. They simply have the user copy someone else's work in hopes of producing an identical result (which is virtually impossible in a classroom full of young children). In this case, the children all have the same pieces, and Vaani expects them to look at the assembled dinosaur and determine where to glue their own pieces to get the same results. This process does not require any creativity; in fact, it discourages individual expression, because the children's dinosaurs will not "look right" unless they place the pieces exactly as Vaani did.

Lost Learning Opportunities

Although Vaani's lesson does teach the children to follow directions, it does not truly teach them art skills. The children have no opportunity to experiment with chalk, paint, crayons, or other media, as Vaani's example does not include them. They also do not get to work with various art tools (paintbrushes, easels, and so on) that would help them develop fine motor skills. They cannot even practice using scissors, because Vaani precut the pieces for them.

After the children assemble their dinosaurs, Vaani posts them on the wall outside the classroom for families to see. As is often the case, the families are thrilled to see and later take home these physical pieces of work that they can save for generations to come. However, they do not see the missed opportunities for learning that occurred in the process of creating the pictures.

Similarly, while a theme can tie all classroom activities together, it can also lead to many duplicated activities with only slight variations. These redundant endeavors take the place of new opportunities for learning.

 Case Study: Sand-Table Struggles

Brent typically has trouble finding a way to link his classroom's sand table to his themes. He often resorts to hiding small plastic toys in the sand, such as woodland creatures for his forest unit and cars for his vehicles unit. Although the children may enjoy finding both types of toys, both activities involve improving fine motor skills. Thus, the children do not really learn anything new at the sand table from one unit to the next, and they may become bored.

At the same time, Brent does not take advantage of certain learning opportunities at the sand table because those activities do not fit any of his themes for the year. For instance, children can learn about volume and measurement by filling measuring cups and other containers with sand, but Brent does not see what this activity has to do with forests, vehicles, or any of his other units. Thus, he views this activity as a waste of time and never offers it to the children.

Incongruity with Children's Interests

Strictly thematic units require that all classroom activities relate to the theme and that the whole class participate, whether or not individual children want to know more about that topic. If preschoolers are not interested in classroom activities, they try to create their own fun—which is usually not the teacher's idea of fun!

 ## Case Study: Insect Unit Gone Wrong

Satina has scheduled a two-week unit on insects for her class. The science center has magnifiers and dead insects that she has found, the library has books such as *The Very Hungry Caterpillar*, and so on. But from the beginning of this unit, several children refuse to participate, squealing, "Ew! Bugs are gross!" To make matters worse, the rest of Satina's class loses interest in the insect activities after just a few days. Satina finds herself dealing with children throwing toys, climbing furniture, wearing books as hats, and exhibiting other challenging behaviors.

Although theme-based units can reinforce concepts by having children use them in each learning center (for instance, putting alphabet blocks in the block center and hiding plastic letters in the sand table), all this interconnected content does no good if the children do not want to participate in the activities. To avoid this problem, monitor the children's interests and rotate classroom materials as those interests change. If you use activities that engage the children, they will learn, whether or not those activities relate to a specific theme.

A Note about Crafts

The point of this section is *not* to say that you should never have children make crafts. Handprint turkeys and so on are fine for an occasional holiday gift, and families will adore them. However, beyond the issues we have already discussed, crafts have some other key drawbacks that make them problematic for everyday lessons:

- With all the available ideas for crafts, you can easily spend more time choosing one than it takes for the children to actually complete one.
- Many crafts require that an adult create pieces (such as cut-out shapes) in advance, a fact that adds a great deal to your workload.
- If a craft is too complicated for the children to complete on their own, you or another adult will have to supervise the entire project, limiting your availability to supervise and assist children in other parts of the classroom.

We explore this issue further in chapter 11.

If Not Theme-Based Units, Then What?

If theme-based units are not the best way to teach young children, then what is? The following principles can guide us:

- Balance thematic and open-ended activities.
- Choose themes that matter to the children.
- Use open-ended materials and conversations.
- Use emergent curriculum to build school readiness.

Balance Thematic and Open-Ended Activities

Thematic units are not bad in and of themselves. In fact, they work well when children have a strong interest in learning about a certain topic. The keys to using themes well are to select them based on the children's interests, not the teacher's, and to avoid making every activity in the classroom focus on a theme. Effective classrooms balance thematic and open-ended activities to maximize learning and problem solving. This practice can help you in several ways.

Engaging Everyone

Not every child in your classroom will want to learn about dinosaurs, transportation, or whatever theme you might choose. Having neutral, creative materials available enables all children to engage in the classroom. This way, the children will always be learning something, regardless of whether they choose to participate in thematic activities.

Avoiding Round Pegs in Square Holes

Some activities, while important to expose children to, typically do not mesh well with themes. For example, color mixing is a typical activity in a preschool classroom. It helps children identify cause and effect as well as learn about the color spectrum. But if you try to force this activity to fit into a theme, you can create more work for yourself without providing any additional benefit to your students.

For example, imagine that your class is learning about how cars can move. To fit a color-mixing activity into this theme, you might cut out thirty or forty construction-paper cars. Then you might have each child put a spoonful of paint on one end of a car, place a spoonful of another color on the opposite end of the car, fold the car in half, and unfold it to look at the results. While this activity does have the children combine colors and does incorporate cars, it offers little else. You have spent a great deal of time cutting out the cars, and the children can see that the colors have mixed. But they do not necessarily understand why or how it has happened, so how much have they really learned?

In contrast, a nonthematic approach to a color-mixing activity would require much less work from you, accomplish the same goals (teaching about cause and effect and about the color spectrum), and even provide some additional benefits. For example, you might place empty ziplock bags on a table along with containers of paint in primary colors. Then you could encourage each child to put two colors into a bag, seal it, and "mush it up" to see what happens. Children love seeing what new colors they create this way, and they get to see the process of the colors combining. Furthermore, by using the bags, you might be able to engage children who typically do not like messy play.

Providing Comfort

Some open-ended materials give comfort to young children simply because they can repeatedly use those items the same way without having to meet any adult expectations. For example, it calms some children to sit and build with wooden blocks with no agenda, so the classroom should provide such options.

Choose Themes That Matter to the Children

When choosing a theme, pick one that is relevant to the children in the classroom. For instance, if a teacher plans a two-week unit on the circus for a classroom of students who have never attended the circus, the children may not engage with that theme. Themes work best when the children have a small amount of knowledge about the topic and desire to learn more. In these cases, once the teacher has selected the theme, she needs to decide which activities should relate to it and which ones should be open-ended. Science and social-studies activities relate well to thematic content; art activities and block play can easily be open-ended.

For example, a unit about hibernation could include flashlight play in the dramatic-play area and science activities about different types of food and how they make the body feel (tired, energetic, and so on). The teacher might choose a book about hibernation for circle time, but she uses the rest of the classroom activities to encourage all children to explore and to help individual children pursue their goals. The classroom library contains books about a variety of topics to appeal to all the children. The art area focuses on learning to use different types of materials, such as fingerpaint or watercolors, instead of on painting pictures of bears or other animals that hibernate.

Use Open-Ended Materials and Conversations

In 2008, researchers at the University of Virginia's Center for Advanced Study of Teaching and Learning (CASTL) developed the *Classroom Assessment Scoring System (CLASS)* for assessing preschool programs. The *CLASS* concentrates on the interactions between students and teachers. Specifically, it guides teachers away from activities that require the children to do something in a specific way to achieve a specific outcome. Instead, it encourages teachers to move toward a culture of asking open-ended questions and brainstorming with the children. These activities, rather than products such as art projects or handwriting samples, become the tools through which adults teach children and measure their learning.

 Case Study: An Unexpected Art Lesson

The current theme for Eliza's classroom is pets, so for today's art activity, she plans on having the students paint with sponges cut into the shapes of dog bones. But when she arrives at school, Eliza realizes that she has left the sponges at home. She has only about fifteen minutes to lay out the day's activities before the children arrive, so she needs to come up with a different art activity. Because she already mixed up the tempera paint yesterday, Eliza decides to use it and lays it, construction paper, and paintbrushes out on the art table. As she moves objects around, she temporarily sets a jar of toothbrushes on the art table. Then she forgets to place the jar back in the cabinet before the school day starts.

Later in the morning, Eliza notices her assistant teacher, Ka'Mya, talking to four-year-old Anthony, who is painting with a paintbrush in one hand and a toothbrush in the other hand. As Eliza moves in closer to hear the conversation, Anthony begins to tell Ka'Mya how the two brushes move differently across the paper:

ANTHONY: (*Moves the paintbrush and then the toothbrush.*) This brush goes whoosh, but this brush can move back and forth and back and forth.

KA'MYA: Why can that brush whoosh?

ANTHONY: (*Makes a smooth motion with the paintbrush.*) It all moves together. My other brush has lots of little groups, but this brush only has one group.

This simple conversation shows that Anthony is beginning to notice significant differences between his two tools. A preestablished art activity may not have allowed him to make the same comparison. When we use simple materials in the classroom and allow children to explore with them, the children typically create their own lessons. Adults can prompt children to examine a situation further and can ask additional questions, but frequently, children's natural curiosity can be the greatest instructor.

Use Loose Parts

To encourage creativity, many preschool classrooms have begun to incorporate loose parts: materials that do not have a specified purpose and that children can use for construction, design, combinations, lining up, and assembly. Loose parts may include wooden spools, stones, sticks, blocks, beads, dried beans, small plastic objects, and much more. Whatever the specific items are, no one tells the children exactly how to use them. Thus, the materials encourage children to create and explore without having to meet certain expectations. Occasionally, children may use loose parts for an art activity that they take home and share with their families, but in many cases, children assemble and disassemble their creations while at school.

These types of materials begin the shift from teacher-directed materials to child-directed materials in the classroom. The more opportunities that children have to decide what to do with materials, the more opportunities they have to practice problem solving.

 ## Case Study: Open-Ended Cardboard Boxes

When Diego arrives in his classroom, he places several empty cardboard boxes in the dramatic-play center. He also places some art materials, such as markers and masking tape, with the boxes. However, he does not specify a play theme or a certain activity for the boxes (such as by saying, "These are your covered wagons so you can go west like pioneers"). The children can create anything they wish from the boxes.

Later that day, the children attempt to create a house with the boxes, and the boxes collapse. Diego prompts the children to think about the problem with questions such as "Why do you think the house fell down?" and "How can you make the house stronger?" These questions help the children create a hypothesis about what happened and allow them to problem solve without specifically directing them to build in any one manner (such as saying, "It needs four walls and a roof").

More Ideas for Open-Ended Materials

Once children begin to experiment with open-ended materials in one or two areas of the classroom, you can expand this idea throughout the classroom. For instance, instead of using only store-bought blocks in the block area, you can add stones, twigs, acorns, and other natural materials (make sure to clean off any dirt or debris first and to have children wash their hands after playing with these items). Children can build with the natural materials separately or alongside store-bought blocks.

This is not to say that you can only use open-ended materials in your classroom. It simply means that if you bring in materials for specific guided activities, you will approach these activities differently than you would in a strictly thematic unit. For example, if Zara wants to help her class learn about materials that sink and materials that float, she might place marbles, plastic blocks, and other objects near the water table. In a strictly thematic unit, she might have the children simply guess whether or not a marble will sink. But if Zara uses both a theme and open-ended activities, she might have one child put a marble in the water and then prompt all the children to hypothesize about why the marble sinks. We want all children, even three- and four-year-olds, to begin using this type of scientific approach to learning.

Every early childhood teacher has the responsibility of encouraging brain development and innovative thinking. Therefore, the entire culture of her classroom must shift from the traditional view that a teacher's job is to tell children what to think or do and how. Instead, she should say things such as, "I wonder what you can do with that sparkly paper." The teacher's focus must change from ensuring perfectly finished products to nurturing children's thinking throughout the day.

Use Emergent Curriculum to Build School Readiness

When we combine all the tips we have discussed in this section—balancing thematic and open-ended activities, choosing themes that matter to the children, and using open-ended materials and conversations—we use a method of teaching known as *emergent curriculum*. The rest of this book explores the details of emergent curriculum and how you can use it to prepare your students so that by the time they begin kindergarten, they will be ready not only to learn literacy and numeracy but also to thrive in a classroom environment.

chapter 2

Emergent Curriculum

What exactly is emergent curriculum? In short, it is a teaching method used to increase creativity in the classroom, meet students' needs, and build school readiness. Emergent curriculum developed from a well-known, successful teaching method called the Reggio Emilia approach. This method was created in Reggio Emilia, Italy, and involves a hands-on approach to teaching and learning. Much as Reggio Emilia teachers do, instead of reusing the same lessons and activities every year, an emergent-curriculum teacher observes each child to find out which topics interest him and which developmental skills he needs to master for kindergarten success. The teacher then blends these components to design activities that not only interest the children but also teach them the skills they need to learn. To this end, the children frequently participate in long-term learning projects that include learning inside and outside the classroom. Each project may focus on one specific topic, but they all incorporate activities that help children build their skills in multiple areas, including the cognitive, language, physical, social-emotional, and self-help domains.

Visit https://www.reggiochildren. it/identita/reggio-emilia-approach/?lang=en to learn more about the Reggio Emilia approach.

What Does an Emergent-Curriculum Classroom Look Like?

An emergent-curriculum classroom does not look strikingly different from most preschool classrooms. However, the classroom operates with intention and direction, even during free-choice time. This component takes up a large portion of each day—at least one uninterrupted hour, but it could be up to three cumulative hours, depending on the classroom schedule. During free-choice time, the children can move throughout the classroom to select materials and learning centers that interest them.

The teacher uses this time to converse with the children and to observe what they do in the classroom. The teacher might use a formal checklist to document his findings or might simply write down notes about each child's skills and interests. Either way, he keeps these records for every child and uses them to plan future lessons. Because lesson plans must include the students' current interests, which can change frequently, the teacher plans only a short time—up to a week—in advance.

Beyond topics that the children enjoy, lesson plans also include opportunities to work on developmental and school-readiness skills that the children need help with. For example, if four or five students struggle to hold a crayon correctly, the teacher might plan one or two activities in the classroom that will help the children build that skill. Not every child has to complete these activities, but the children who need them can access them. On the other hand, if some students need harder challenges because they can already write all their letters, the teacher might provide supplies for those children to write letters during a variety of activities. For instance, the teacher can put paper and pencils in the dramatic-play area for children to write shopping lists while pretending to go to the grocery store, or he might include writing materials in the block area so children can describe the types of towers they build.

In an emergent-curriculum classroom, activities can involve using multiple skills at the same time. For example, an activity in the dramatic-play area may include chances to develop language by having a conversation, strengthen fine motor skills by dressing up, and practice cooperation by creating a group story line. Though formal assessments often require that teachers document children's individual skills, emergent curriculum encourages teaching the whole child. Notably, adults commonly work on projects that use skills from multiple categories of learning, such as writing code for software (which involves understanding computer operations and cause and effect) or devising a new marketing campaign (which uses expressive-language skills and art design). Therefore, children need to have similarly multifaceted classroom experiences from a young age.

Project-based learning often requires interdisciplinary work, so projects are a staple of emergent curriculum. In preschool, *project-based learning* means that the children focus most of their activities on learning about one specific topic. A project could last from a few days to several weeks or months. During each project, the teachers learn with the children about new topics and adjust classroom activities based on the children's developing interests.

For example, if the children want to learn about baking, the teacher can turn this interest into a project that helps them also learn math, science, and reading concepts. Children learn aspects of literacy when they see the teacher read a recipe and follow the directions step by step. When the children help measure the ingredients, they learn higher-level math skills. Mixing and baking the ingredients teaches the children about cause and effect as individual ingredients combine into one new item, especially because a final baked product often looks completely different from its batter.

The teacher uses the lesson-planning process to make sure that he meets program and state requirements and families' needs. He has a responsibility to prepare children for kindergarten, so he needs to include certain lessons in the curriculum, such as writing letters of the alphabet or identifying shapes and colors. However, he does not have to teach these concepts through rote learning, such as by asking children to identify shapes and colors on flash cards. When children simply memorize information, they may not be able to apply those concepts to real-world examples. For instance, a red circle on a flash card will look different from a blush-red apple or a deep-red sunset. To make this type of learning both engaging and more readily applicable to the real world, the teacher can incorporate it into projects or games that capture the children's interests. He might, for instance, play I Spy with the children so they can search for real-life red items throughout the classroom or on the playground.

In the same manner, the teacher takes the needs of families into account in his lesson plans. If Ainsley's family expresses a strong desire that she learn to write her name before kindergarten, her teacher should make that goal part of the curriculum. But he does not necessarily need to make Ainsley sit at a table and practice writing again and again. While Ainsley will eventually need some of this type of practice, the teacher will likely have better success if he offers activities that Ainsley likes that also help her build the skills she needs for writing. (We further explore the development of writing skills in chapter 9.)

Many teachers wonder how children will behave if they get to choose their activities and where to play. Understandably, adults may fear that their classrooms will descend into chaos. But in general, when children are engaged in activities and projects that interest them, behavior problems significantly decrease. On the other hand, if many children lose interest in classroom activities, the teacher needs to review the lesson plan and select new activities.

What Emergent Curriculum Is Not

Emergent curriculum does not include certain characteristics that are common in many early childhood curricula. Emergent curriculum has no designated beginning or end point. The lessons are not strictly theme based or planned more than a week in advance. The curriculum is not predictable, because it grows out of the continuously changing needs and interests of a distinct group of students. Therefore, emergent curriculum is rarely repetitive—although it can be if the children fixate on one topic—so it does not often become boring for children or adults. If the children begin to show a lack of interest, the teacher can easily move on to a new topic.

Teacher Responsibilities in Emergent Curriculum

In many preschool classrooms, everything centers on the teacher. The teacher entertains the children during an extended circle time and selects themes and activities that have worked well in previous school years. Emergent curriculum changes this dynamic, because children initiate and direct their own learning with adult assistance. They select topics that they want to learn about and learning centers that engage them, and adults help as needed. This can mean that the teacher engages one child in a back-and-forth conversation in the dramatic-play area, searches the internet with another child to research the fastest land animal, or watches at the art table while a third child uses loose parts to create a model of a cheetah.

Let's look at some of a teacher's specific responsibilities in emergent curriculum.

Documenting and Assessing Children's Learning

In emergent-curriculum classrooms, teachers must devote large amounts of time to documentation and assessment. Many programs already use *TeachingStrategies GOLD*, administer other regularly scheduled assessments, or require teachers to have certain documentation and evaluations on file before parent-teacher conferences. But in emergent curriculum, teachers document and assess children's skills throughout the school day, particularly during free-choice time. This data forms the backbone of all classroom planning; teachers cannot complete their weekly lesson plans without it.

This method may sound like much more work than quarterly or conference-time assessments, but it works similarly to straightening a room a little bit every day instead of deep-cleaning it once every few months or right before company arrives. Because documentation and assessment form a part of daily routines, these tasks do not pile up for teachers to complete after school or at the end of each quarter. This style of assessment also helps improve teaching by giving educators constant access to data that shows what the children need.

Explaining Emergent Curriculum to Families

Because children's families may not understand the style of learning in emergent curriculum, the teacher needs to advocate for *child-led learning experiences*, or classroom learning activities selected based on the children's learning interests. He must articulate why and how this type of learning prepares children for kindergarten and why creation, problem solving, and language interaction work better than rote memorization. Using his daily notes and assessments, the teacher can show families how their children have grown over time through participating in emergent curriculum. If the teacher has well-developed communication skills and can advocate for emergent curriculum, family members will more likely accept this teaching method and begin to participate in the classroom.

Talking with Children

The teacher uses conversations with students to help them develop theories about how the world works. He encourages the children to express their ideas, and he uses those thoughts to guide the children to develop hypotheses. If DeMarcus is painting at an easel, the teacher might ask, "Why do you think the paint is dripping down your paper?" If Esperanza is placing counting bears on a block, the teacher could inquire, "How do the bears choose their seats?" If Keith is playing with slime or playdough, the teacher might say, "What does that feel like when you touch it?"

Shaping the Learning Environment

Rather than connecting everything in the classroom to the current theme, the teacher creates a learning environment that encourages children to play and explore with the learning materials. In every area of the classroom, he stores materials in such a way that children can easily access them without adult assistance. Children should always have access to quiet areas in the classroom, so the teacher arranges the room to keep social, noisy areas (such as the block area and the dramatic-play area) away from areas that encourage quiet time or individual learning (such as the classroom library).

The classroom and its resources have just as great an effect on creating a learning environment as the planned activities do. When children have many different learning materials to choose from, they can choose to play with the materials that engage them and can repeat that play to build their skills. As children develop skill mastery and a sense of ownership in classroom activities, they become more confident and form a sense of self-worth. They begin to develop their identities as they learn about their capabilities and talents. All these outcomes move the classroom toward providing better education and a loving environment for the students. If a child feels safe to try out new things throughout the classroom, then he willingly takes chances to learn new things.

Observing and Identifying Children's Needs

The teacher does not do much direct teaching—that is, sitting the children down and telling them to complete an activity in a certain way—in an emergent-curriculum classroom. But he remains extremely busy taking notes and participating in activities with the children. Emergent curriculum encourages the teacher to observe all the children so he can get to know each student on a deep level, well beyond favorite colors and family members' names. Through this process, the teacher discovers what each child knows, what makes him curious, what motivates him, and which skills he has already mastered.

As he makes these discoveries, the teacher can no longer assume that all students are ready to learn the same skills or will learn them at the same time. He begins to see each child as a competent, curious expert in his (the child's) own right, an individual who approaches new challenges in his own time and sequence and therefore has unique goals.

 Case Study: Capitalizing on Rashawn's Interest

Four-year-old Rashawn knows the name of each species of toy dinosaur in the classroom but does not yet know letter names. He shows obvious curiosity and great potential for learning. To engage Rashawn, his teacher, Imani, plans activities that encourage Rashawn's interest in dinosaurs and help him to make hypotheses about what the dinosaur world was like.

Imani recognizes that Rashawn's fascination can help him learn in unexpected ways. For instance, his large vocabulary of dinosaur names will assist him when he is eventually motivated to learn letter names. Children with large vocabularies frequently have an easier time sounding words out as they learn to read, because they already have a basis for comparison. If Rashawn is familiar with, say, the name *T. rex* when he begins to sound it out, he can compare the individual letter sounds to the store of words in his memory and more quickly associate the sounds with a word he knows. Additionally, Rashawn's exposure to creating hypotheses will assist him in developing more advanced problem-solving skills as he works through the process of identifying a problem, making a logical guess about a solution, and testing out the guess to see whether it is correct.

Promoting Lifelong Learning

Emergent curriculum encourages lifelong learning for both the teacher and the students. A teacher in this type of classroom must willingly continue learning instead of sticking to the units that he may have taught for years. At first, he may know little about the content that the children want to explore. That is okay; he does not need to be an expert to help them learn. The teacher can set an example for his students by admitting that he does not know everything but is willing to learn. Then they all can do research together to find out how dams produce energy, how long it takes a tree to grow, how the internet works, or whatever else the children want to know. By using the learning process in the classroom and learning alongside the students, the teacher does not have to spend additional time outside of school to research the topic.

Emergent curriculum can promote lifelong learning among children's families, too. When children come home excited about what they are learning at school, that knowledge spills over into the lives of their family members. Family members might already know about the topic their child has been studying, but the child might also teach the rest of the family something new.

The Planning Cycle

Once the teacher gathers information about his students, he uses that data to decide what lessons or activities to bring into the classroom next. This planning method uses a four-step process:

1. Analyze observation notes.
2. Determine activities and goals for students.
3. Implement activities and teach students how to participate.
4. Evaluate the students' progress in building skills.

While this process may sound complicated, it is actually simple.

Step 1: Analyze Observation Notes

To analyze his observation notes, the teacher reviews them in search of specific information. He looks for evidence about which skills the children have mastered and which skills need more time and attention. He seeks clues about how his students learn, including activities that motivate each child and which learning styles (active, visual, or auditory) each child prefers. Last but not least, the teacher hunts for topics of interest to the children—things they talk about frequently, common story lines in their play, and so on.

Step 2: Determine Activities and Goals for Students

Once he has analyzed the data, the teacher uses the results to plan activities for the next week. Sometimes the children's interest in a topic lasts several weeks, but because the teacher cannot know for sure which topics will spark this level of fascination, he plans only one week at a time.

 Case Study: From Observation to Activities

As Keri analyzes her most recent set of observation notes, she notices a pattern. Everyone in her class can use a palmar grasp (a full-hand grasp), but only two children can use a tripod grasp (a grasp with the thumb, index, and middle fingers). She knows that all the children need to master the tripod grasp so they can eventually learn to write.

As Keri thinks about how to help the children practice the tripod grasp, she recalls that easel painting makes it difficult to use a palmar grasp on a paintbrush. Because of the angle at which the easel places the paper, a child must reposition his hand into a tripod grasp in order to manipulate a paintbrush. Keri decides to add some easels to the art area. Also, because a tripod grasp requires extra strength in three of the five fingers, Keri decides to set up some tables where the children can play clothespin games and use playdough, two fine motor activities that will increase their finger strength.

Step 3: Implement Activities and Teach Students How to Participate

Each time the teacher introduces an activity to the classroom, he teaches the children how to participate. First, he models the activity for everyone during circle time. Then, when the children have the chance to try the activity on their own, he observes them to determine what, if any, extra support each child needs. Some children may catch on simply by watching the teacher model an activity, while others may need hand-over-hand assistance for their first attempts at that activity.

Step 4: Evaluate Students' Progress in Building Skills

As the teacher observes students participating in activities, he can work out how much practice the children will need to master the skills taught in each activity. Some children lose interest in an activity before they have mastered the applicable skill, so the teacher may need to rotate materials frequently to keep the children engaged while they build the skill. He also watches to determine when a child has mastered a skill and is ready to work on more-complicated ones.

In emergent curriculum, no learning experiences are accidental. The children learn through play, and the teacher prepares both the children and the environment to allow for those learning opportunities. Each step of the planning cycle provides new information about the students, and the teacher analyzes that information and uses it to enhance the learning environment.

Timing in Theme-Based vs. Emergent Curriculum

When we compare emergent curriculum to theme-based teaching, one of the biggest differences is timing. Many preschool teachers habitually operate on a two-week timetable, spending exactly two weeks on each unit and thereby giving the children exactly two weeks to master the associated skills. However, this pattern means that teachers may change their focus before the children are ready to move on, or they may spend so much time on a topic that the children lose interest. Emergent curriculum, on the other hand, moves at the children's pace. Emergent curriculum can cover the same amount of content as a theme-based curriculum, but emergent curriculum does not fit neatly into two-week packages. Depending on their interests and existing abilities, children might take a long time to master some skills and master others more quickly.

Support for Ongoing Projects

An emergent-curriculum classroom allows children to start large projects that might take multiple days or weeks to complete. This way, the children do not have to rush through their learning, particularly when they have a strong interest in a certain subject. In addition, they begin to develop reasonable expectations for how long certain tasks will take.

The teacher must create a culture in which children feel safe leaving their unfinished projects out to complete later. To establish this type of trust, he allows students to start projects daily, and he sets and enforces rules about touching only one's own projects. Some teachers create "safe spaces" in their classrooms where children can place unfinished projects. Other teachers set up safe spaces around children's creations, such as by using crepe paper to rope off the area of the block center that contains an in-progress tower.

To establish the specific procedures for his classroom, the teacher sits down with the children at circle time and asks them how everyone can protect unfinished projects at the end of each day. If students contribute to creating the procedure, they feel invested in it and are much more likely to participate.

Common Misconceptions about Emergent Curriculum

Although emergent curriculum has much to offer for both the students and the teachers, many early childhood programs choose not to use this type of curriculum because of common misconceptions about it. Let's address some of these erroneous beliefs.

Misconception 1: "We Already Have a Curriculum"

One of the most common objections to emergent curriculum sounds something like this: "I can't do emergent curriculum because my program uses a different curriculum, and I'm required to follow that." In fact, you can incorporate emergent curriculum into your teaching no matter what curriculum you already use. We explore this challenge in depth in chapter 4.

Misconception 2: "There *Is* No Plan!"

Another common misconception about emergent curriculum is that the teacher does not plan activities in advance for the children. Instead, according to this theory, the children "get to do whatever they want," and the teacher simply waits to see what they want to play with and then joins in. This misconception can make emergent curriculum seem more like babysitting than creating a structured learning environment. It may also cause teachers and administrators to worry about whether they can use emergent curriculum and still cover the content required by local, state, or national preschool standards.

The root of this misconception may lie in the timelines for lesson planning in different curricula. Many teachers in traditional preschool classrooms begin working on their lesson plans months ahead of time. These plans may involve a great deal of thought. But when teachers plan so far in advance, they cannot know exactly what the children will need or be interested in by the time that lesson comes around. Instead, teachers often plan by selecting topics and activities that they enjoy doing with the children, not necessarily the activities that the children need to help them move to the next stage of development.

Emergent-curriculum teachers plan closer to the time of implementation, because young children's interests—and, therefore, the basis of a lesson—can change quickly. Though emergent-curriculum lessons may seem much less structured than lessons from other curricula, the emergent-curriculum teacher uses the data he gathers each day to create his

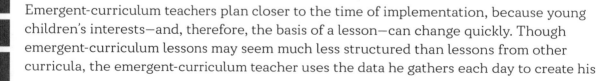

lessons with intention. The lesson plans allow the children some exploration instead of scripting out exactly what everyone should do during the course of the lesson. The plans also address skills that the current group of children is prepared to master, instead of trying to make a lesson plan from a previous year work for a completely different set of individuals.

 ## Case Study: Planning Too Far Ahead

Paul has taught preschool for over seven years, and he has developed many lesson-plan resources. Some of his past students' favorite learning units include transportation and dinosaurs, so he uses these units every winter, when the children cannot go outside as often, in hopes of keeping them more engaged. Typically, Paul will get out the materials for these units over the winter break and rewrite them slightly for the months of January and February.

When Paul begins planning his transportation unit this year, he knows that most of his students cannot write their first names, so he focuses on using many of the transportation activities to teach that skill. For instance, he plans to have the children "drive" small toy cars through paint and use the cars to write their names. To provide models for this activity, he "car writes" each child's first name on a large piece of paper and laminates it. As he usually does, Paul intends to begin the transportation unit during the last week of January and continue it for three weeks.

When Paul's students come back from winter break in early January, several of them have learned to write their first names. With these new peer role models, the other children show great interest in writing their own first names with paper and pencils. They spend so much time on this skill that by the time Paul's unit on transportation begins, the children have largely mastered writing their first names and now want to learn to write their last names. Paul's "car writing" activity no longer relates to the children's current interests and abilities.

 ## Case Study: Helping "Veterinarians" Prepare for Writing

Andrea typically waits to plan her lessons until one week in advance. She keeps up-to-date notes on the children's developmental skills by using her *TeachingStrategies GOLD* assessment data. Based on her observations, Andrea knows that her students are not ready to learn to write their names, so she wants to help them work on their pencil grips first.

Andrea also listens to what the children talk about so she can identify their interests. This year, the students constantly talk about their pets. Many of them have told Andrea they want to be veterinarians when they grow up. Lately, the children have been pretending to be veterinarians in the dramatic-play area.

One day, Andrea asks the children in this center if they have ever seen an X-ray. None of them has. Andrea explains that an X-ray is a picture of the inside of a pet's body without the skin. The children show great interest in this topic, asking question after question about X-rays.

Andrea brainstorms how to connect this fascination to her goal of helping the children practice their pencil grips. She invents an entertaining way to use easel drawing. The next week, Andrea brings in several boxes to be X-ray machines, and she tapes a large piece of paper to one side of each box. She places a variety of writing tools, such as pencils and markers, in the dramatic-play area. She tells the children that they can use the boxes like easels to draw X-rays of the classroom's stuffed animals. Because Andrea provides several boxes, several children can engage in the activity at once. The children are so interested in being veterinarians that this activity stays very popular for over two weeks.

Misconception 3: "The Children Run the Classroom"

People often describe emergent curriculum as a child-led curriculum. This terminology makes some teachers nervous. They feel that if they let children lead, the teachers will lose control of the planning—and everything else—in their classrooms.

In emergent curriculum, teachers do need to relinquish the desire to personally select the subject of each lesson. They find great fulfillment, after all, in studying things that interest both them and the children. However, young children find interest in many subjects, so over the course of several years, teachers will likely plan lessons that cover every topic they personally desire to explore. Furthermore, far from children running amok, emergent curriculum provides two somewhat surprising benefits. First, it can significantly reduce negative student behaviors, because the students remain interested in the classroom activities instead of becoming bored and testing boundaries. Second, the emergent-curriculum classroom teaches the teachers as well as the students. Emergent-curriculum teachers can learn something new each day at work, so they do not burn out as quickly as teachers who repeat the same lesson plans every year.

 Case Study: So Much for Dinosaurs

Fiona has mapped out a two-week unit on dinosaurs for her class, only to discover that the children have little interest in this topic. She seemingly has to throw out the entire unit. However, despite appearances, the children have not hijacked the schedule. Fiona can still use many, if not all, of her planned activities; she might simply have to change their focus to match the children's current interests, or she might have to save certain activities for a time when the children show interest in dinosaurs. The following are a few examples of what Fiona could do.

- Fiona has collected small plastic dinosaurs to place in the sand table for a "paleontology dig." Because the children currently love superheroes, which do not make much sense as part of a paleontology dig, Fiona chooses to save this activity for later.
- The children have greatly enjoyed using the dinosaur-shaped stamps that Fiona has added to the art center, and holding the stamps has helped them work on their pincer grasps (thumb and index finger) and tripod grasps (thumb, index finger, and middle finger). Fiona decides to bring in additional stamps shaped like popular superheroes.
- During her observations of the classroom, Fiona listens to the children's conversations to see what the students like and when they might want to learn about dinosaurs. If and when they display this interest, she will be ready.
- One student, Hannah, does show interest in dinosaurs. To provide her with individualized attention—and to gauge whether other children might be interested in this topic—Fiona offers Hannah some of the dinosaur activities.

Misconception 4: "This Is *Way* Too Much Work"

Another myth about the emergent-curriculum classroom stems from a misunderstanding of why teachers collect observations on each child and do not reuse lesson plans from year to year. Some people believe that teachers must use their observation data to create new activities or projects for every interest of every child in the classroom. Understandably, this idea can feel overwhelming, especially given how quickly children's interests change. They can jump from superheroes to jungle animals to ninjas to fire trucks, sometimes all in the same week—and that may be just one child!

The good news is that teachers do not have to invent an activity for every interest. In many—if not most—cases, one activity can engage numerous children because they all share a certain interest or need to work on the same skill. Of course, in a room of twenty preschoolers, it is challenging to plan an activity that appeals to everyone. But emergent curriculum uses two strategies to manage this challenge.

First, as he works individually with each child, the teacher not only tracks the child's development but gets to know him and finds out what motivates him. Then, if a child does not have a natural desire to participate in an activity, the teacher can use what he has learned to find a way to spark that child's interest. This technique can simplify classroom management by leading more children to participate in the same activity.

Still, not every child will want to participate in every activity or help with every project. This leads to the second technique: instead of planning twenty individual lessons per day to address the interests of each child, the teacher simply needs to spend individual time with students who do not show as much interest in the classroom activities or projects. This way, teachers can customize minilessons to these children so they can still learn the same concepts or content as they would by participating in the larger-group effort.

Case Study: Teaching James One-on-One

Tahlia's class is doing a project on building robots as a way to problem solve, learn new vocabulary, and think creatively. Most students excitedly use the loose-parts section of the classroom to construct their own robots. However, James chooses to play alone in the block area, pretending to move the blocks with cranes and tow trucks. Tahlia watches him for a while and realizes that James has a strong interest in construction equipment. She adds some small construction trucks to the block area and talks with James about which truck can carry the heaviest load. This leads to an excellent discussion on why one truck can carry more weight than another.

Overall, Tahlia's goal is not to teach each child about robots. Her goal is to use a topic that interests the children to help them master specific school-readiness skills. Most of the children do so through the robot project. James does it through his discussion with Tahlia. In both cases, Tahlia has found an interesting way to help the children work on their creative thinking, vocabulary, and problem solving.

Ideas for Including Everyone in Projects

When choosing topics and projects, the teacher should select ones that appeal to as many of his students as possible. However, multiple projects can occur in a classroom at the same time. For instance, while most of the children work on a mural, a small group may choose to create masks. If this smaller project captures the interest of children from the larger group, it may lead the class to its next unit of study.

One important goal of any project is to teach students how to focus on topics that interest them and how to pursue additional learning on those topics. Once a child knows how to pursue his own learning, he can explore his chosen topic independently, even if the rest of the class is working on other projects. Because most preschoolers cannot read well enough to use books or the internet to do research on their own, they need adults to show them other ways to pursue their own learning while they build their literacy skills. For instance, the teacher could encourage children to ask questions, look at picture books, perform experiments, or do research with his assistance.

Benefits of Emergent Curriculum

Although it does take a significant amount of time to customize lessons to children's interests, emergent curriculum provides many benefits. First, teachers and students can often learn together, because the children may be interested in topics that the teacher

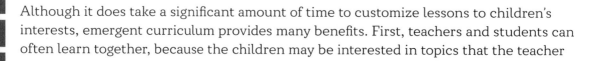

knows little about. Though the teacher should plan lessons ahead of time, he does not have to prepare all the materials in advance; he can explore topics in the classroom alongside the children.

Second, when children learn about a topic that interests them, behavior problems in the classroom significantly decrease. Challenging behaviors typically emerge when children become bored with the materials or concepts in a lesson and try to find something more interesting to do. When the children can select what they want to learn about, they are motivated to participate in acceptable classroom activities—exactly the behavior that teachers want. Teachers can then work with the children on learning instead of having to constantly redirect negative behaviors. This change can take a heavy burden off teachers.

Finally, emergent curriculum greatly reduces the amount of work the teacher must do for art activities. DIY-style art projects often require extensive preparations by the teacher, such as cutting out premade pieces. But when individual children select what type of art to create, they, not the teacher, become responsible for the artistic process. Art making happens in real time instead of happening largely outside of school hours. Additionally, when the teacher hangs up unique pieces of artwork instead of a classroom full of matching creations, he does not need to prepare additional decorations to create a perfectly themed bulletin board.

In short, an emergent-curriculum teacher greatly reduces his workload by simply empowering the children to learn about what they enjoy.

Misconception 5: "Emergent Curriculum, Project Approach—Same Thing"

Emergent curriculum is often compared to the Project Approach, in which children frequently do research and complete projects on topics they are curious about. Similarly, an emergent-curriculum classroom often has this type of work going on. However, the Project Approach uses a highly defined structure

> Visit http://projectapproach.org/ about/project-approach/ to learn more about the Project Approach.

and series of steps to develop and execute projects, and the teacher might suggest topics for them. Emergent curriculum, which is more organic, emphasizes that projects should stem from children's interests. Thus, if the children are not currently showing curiosity about a specific topic, they might not be working on a project and might simply be completing other learning activities. This is fine. The point of emergent curriculum is for children to explore their interests, not for them to always have a project underway.

Classroom displays also vary slightly between Project Approach classrooms and emergent-curriculum classrooms. A Project Approach classroom often displays artwork or writing related to the current whole-class project, although the individual pieces of work will not be identical. Other displays may highlight group work related to the project, such as a robot that the children have constructed together. An emergent-curriculum classroom might use these types of displays if the children are currently working on a project, or the room might simply have various learning centers set up throughout the space.

A typical Project Approach classroom has all the children participate in the same project, but a typical emergent-curriculum classroom has multiple small-group activities going on at any given time. Just as Megan created an impromptu inclined-plane lesson with the three boys in the introduction, the teacher in an emergent-curriculum classroom frequently supports children's learning interests by helping the children create their own experiments or art in real time.

chapter 3

The Importance of Play

Free play, also known as *undirected play* or *open-ended play* (hereafter simply *play*) is an essential part of any preschool classroom, particularly an emergent-curriculum classroom. Specifically, play is an activity in which children interact with classroom materials and other students in spontaneous, open-ended ways. An adult does not step in to require a certain outcome for the play—for example, instructing the children to set up a doctor's office in the dramatic-play area or to research caterpillars in the science center. Children must still follow the social rules of the classroom, such as maintaining safety and showing courtesy to their peers. But within those boundaries, they can explore the classroom and its materials and use their own creativity to construct whatever story or outcome they can imagine.

Why Play Is Essential

Over time, many adults have adopted the view that playtime and learning time are two separate activities. But for young children, playtime *is* learning time. Renowned early childhood researcher Maria Montessori explains play as "the work of the young child."

Play attracts children not just because it is enjoyable but also because it is purposeful. Play involves intentionally exploring one's environment, interacting with people, and experimenting with objects. Through these activities, a child learns about the world and how it works. For example, when a child puts together a puzzle, she learns about perspective and how different shapes fit or do not fit together. When she pretends to be a monster and chases her friends, she learns about social rules and the differences between reality and fantasy.

Unfortunately for play, the culture of American education has changed significantly over the past ten to fifteen years. Society now prioritizes introducing academic skills at younger ages to improve school readiness. Because teachers and schools are expected to keep children sitting at desks for long periods of academic instruction, caregivers have noticed that children are not developing some essential skills—ones that they typically learn through play.

According to an article by Kenneth Ginsburg, the Committee on Communications, and the Committee on Psychosocial Aspects of Child and Family Health, play benefits all areas of a child's development: cognitive, social, emotional, physical, and language. A child's language skills begin to grow as she plays with other children and learns to communicate her wants and needs. When children move through the classroom and playground by crawling, walking, jumping, and climbing, their motor skills start to improve. Dramatic play allows children to develop empathy for others by observing their points of view in the invented scenarios.

Let's look in greater depth at some other benefits of play.

Forming Healthy Habits

When children engage in physical play—such as climbing, playing chase, or jumping rope—at least twice a day, they begin to develop physical maturity and lifelong healthy habits. By learning to explore their environments to seek out information (versus waiting for information to come to them, as happens during activities such as watching television), children develop patterns that can help them avoid a passive lifestyle. Physical play also assists in developing the sensory system, which plays a crucial role in a child's ability to take in information through the senses and process that information in the brain. In particular, gross motor play allows children to feel their bodies move through space and to begin to physically relate to the world around them.

Providing Safe Places for Emotional Expression

Play gives children a safe environment in which to express their emotions. In particular, the dramatic-play area of the classroom can allow children to imitate emotions they have seen at home or to act out conversations they have witnessed. When children have to sit and listen for extended periods, they must often internalize their emotions, because this type of setting is not the appropriate place to express them. In a play-based setting, on the other hand, children can play alone if they need time to themselves, and they can utilize dramatic play with their friends as an outlet for and a method to identify their emotions. If a child is angry, for example, you may notice her speaking firmly to a baby doll about why it will not go to sleep. Such dramatic-play scenarios often mirror situations that a child has seen or been part of at home, especially if she does not know how to handle her emotional responses to these situations. Play allows children to face their fears by exploring or acting them out without the stress of real-life negative outcomes. They can model adult roles in the home and work out how they will eventually behave when they have the opportunity to make certain choices.

Encouraging Experimentation and Exploration

Play allows children to experiment and explore, the same skills that they will use later to study science. In an emergent-curriculum classroom, children have opportunities to determine how things work and whether they (the children) can change outcomes. Play allows children to analyze a problem and test out a solution. If a block tower falls, the children can create a hypothesis about why it fell and then test out that theory when they rebuild the tower. These same types of experiments cannot occur when a child sits at a desk with paper and pencil.

Building Social and Emotional Skills

During free play, children can share, negotiate with one another, resolve their own problems, and build friendships. Play also encourages children to build decision-making skills, and when they make an independent decision in a group setting, they develop self-confidence. When they do not successfully make a decision, they begin creating a new plan for their next attempt. Play also allows children to develop their leadership skills and their creativity. You might, for instance, see one child creating the story line in the dramatic-play area and instructing other students about how they can all participate. This is a child's opportunity to learn how to develop ideas, encourage others to join in, and not demand too much from peers.

The Decline of Play

Some adults assume that children get enough playtime simply because they are children and that play should therefore not be a large focus area in preschool. However, children today actually have far fewer opportunities to play than adults may realize. This happens partly because of a dramatic increase in technology. Instead of building bedroom forts and going on backyard "bear hunts," many children come home after school or child care and simply sit in front of a screen. The computer, tablet, phone, or television provides the story line and directions for how to participate in the experience, so the child has no need to be creative or explore. This is also a sedentary style of learning, as children do not run, chase, or build physical objects in these activities.

Other children may participate in structured games and lessons, such as soccer practices, ballet classes, or piano lessons. These children do learn, build motor skills (even piano lessons strengthen finger and arm muscles), and avoid screen time. However, these types of activities do not encourage the same levels of imagination and problem solving as unstructured play does. In a practice, class, or lesson setting, a coach or teacher gives the child direct instruction about what to do next. This interaction can build a child's ability to focus and learn a skill, but it should be complemented with unstructured time in the child's schedule.

Many preschools also introduce some type of homework to young children. Again, this type of activity can develop skills in following directions and focusing, but it does not improve social skills, imagination, and problem solving in the same manner as play. Completing a worksheet at home requires that the child follow several steps in rote order, but problem solving is a more advanced skill in which a child learns to apply skills, steps, and processes to multiple situations. For example, when two children problem solve about how they can both have a turn to feed a baby doll in the dramatic-play area, they not only work on their problem-solving skills but also develop their creativity and social skills.

Because of the overall cultural decline in play, some children enter preschool without understanding how to explore an environment and play independently. They wait for direct instruction from a teacher or a computer to prompt their learning. In these cases, teachers and family members need to sit down with the children and model exploratory and imaginative play. For example, a teacher can create a block tower and ask a child who lives in there and what those people do each day. Family members can build couch-cushion forts with their children and "protect" their structures from a dreaded "dragon." Children need to participate in these types of guided imaginative experiences to learn how to brainstorm their own creative adventures.

The Benefits of Dramatic Play

Dramatic play, also known as *imaginative play*, *symbolic play*, or *pretend play*, occurs when a child pretends to be someone else to act out thoughts and dreams. The child can dress up or role-play using small toys. When children dress up, they typically use a wide variety of props and tools to act out their fantasies. A child may dress up in an apron and pretend to work in the kitchen with a whisk, or she may use that apron as a suit of armor and the whisk as her trusty sword. The environment and the props do not have to resemble the story line, because in dramatic play, the child creates her own version of reality. She can invite her friends to participate in her story, or she can act out her story on her own.

Social and Emotional Development

One of the greatest benefits of dramatic play is that it gives young children an opportunity to make sense of the world around them. They can act out the same scenes and stories again and again until they begin to understand why the characters behave the way that they do. As part of this process, children may reenact an argument they have seen at home, or they may pretend to be the princes and princesses they have seen in a storybook. When children act out their pretend scenes, they attempt to mirror the characters' emotions. They learn to identify others' facial expressions and emotions, and then they begin to distinguish among the emotions they personally experience.

Group dramatic play helps children begin to develop skills for leadership and other social interactions. When one child takes the lead in this type of play, she must learn to listen to and perceive the needs of others in the group. Collaborative play helps children build friendships and learn to follow social rules. As children act out their stories, they typically share costumes, take turns creating the plot, and negotiate compromises when they disagree ("There are only three bears in the story, but you can be Goldilocks").

Language Development

Language skills significantly increase during group dramatic play. To explain to their peers what should happen next in a story and to communicate their needs, children need to build their language skills. Their vocabulary increases to express the intricacies of each story. Their listening skills improve as other children in the group explain their characters and add twists to each plot. Children also learn cultural norms and new ways to use language as their classmates act out stories from their own homes.

Fine Motor Development

Dramatic play helps young children improve their fine motor skills. Dress-up play gives children practice dressing and undressing (also an important self-help skill) using snaps, zippers, and Velcro. If a child uses small blocks and action figures for dramatic play, she learns to manipulate small pieces. She strengthens the muscles in her arms, hands, and fingers as she creates forts, builds backdrops, and arranges props.

How Teachers Can Help

To help children gain the benefits of dramatic play, the teacher must establish a classroom environment that encourages this type of play. First, she can model dramatic-play skills and participate in this type of play with the children. She also needs to observe the children to discover their needs and interests so she can provide relevant dramatic-play materials. For instance, if the children gravitate toward dress-up clothing, the teacher needs to provide plenty of costumes for them to share. If children often participate in dramatic play in the block center, the teacher needs to provide a variety of blocks and props in that area. Rather than forcing a specific dramatic-play theme on the children ("We're learning about the beach this week, so we should play that"), she should provide multiple kinds of materials so the children can choose among many themes.

The Benefits of Messy Play

Messy play, also known as *sensory play*, allows children to engage their curiosity and take in a great deal of information through multiple sensory systems, especially the tactile system. In a typical early childhood classroom, messy play might involve using playdough, fingerpaint, a sand or water table, or a mud kitchen. Messy play allows children to learn through having messy experiences and experimenting with the results.

Motor Development

Messy play has many benefits for children's overall growth and development, but it has a particularly strong effect on motor development. Children manipulate messy materials such as clay and slime with their hands. These motions can refine many of the muscles in the fingers, wrists, arms, and even shoulders. Children also develop coordination from using tools such as cookie cutters and rolling pins to manipulate materials. These developments assist with a child's later ability to hold and manipulate a pencil.

Gross motor skills can also benefit from messy play. Outdoor activities such as jumping in puddles, blowing bubbles, and moving sand around in a sandbox can activate and strengthen large muscles in the legs, torso, and arms. When large muscles act as support for the smaller muscles in the body (for example, the arm supporting the hand while a child paints on an easel), children can achieve a higher level of balance and muscle control.

Sensory Development

Messy play helps develop the body's sensory systems. Typically, we think of the human body as having five main senses: taste, touch, smell, sight, and hearing. But when thinking about overall sensory development for a young child, we also need to consider the vestibular and proprioceptive senses.

The *vestibular sense* controls the body's awareness of movement and balance. A child with a well-developed vestibular system has good balance, coordination, and equilibrium. A child with an underdeveloped vestibular system may seem awkward and clumsy. Just as messy play can help children build their gross motor skills, it can also help them develop their vestibular senses by, for example, running in sand, painting with bare feet, and working with modeling clay.

The *proprioceptive sense* identifies where one's body is in space and what it needs to do next. The skin, muscles, and joints all contain receptors that take in proprioceptive information. The brain uses that information to determine where the body is, how it is moving, and how much strength the muscles need to exert. This sense helps control muscle movement and posture. If a child's proprioceptive system does not work well, she may appear clumsy (similar to a child with vestibular difficulties), or she may use inappropriate amounts of muscle control. For example, she may run and crash into things unnecessarily or kick a ball extremely hard when a small tap would suffice. Messy play, particularly in outdoor environments, gives children the opportunity to practice muscle movements and to master coordination and postural skills.

One of the most important benefits of messy play is that it builds neural connections in the brain that enable a child to complete more-complex activities. This neural growth occurs for two reasons. First, during messy play, multiple sensory systems are involved in the learning process and taking in different types of information. For instance, when a child plays with shaving cream, she sees the cream swirling and squishing around, hears the noises it makes as she touches and moves it, smells its unique scent, and feels its thick, foamy consistency. Second, messy play improves fine motor skills. It typically involves manipulating materials with the hands, which often cross the midline of the body in the process, such as when a child uses the same hand to finger-paint a horizontal line across her entire paper. When body parts cross the midline, the two halves of the brain must communicate more with one another than when a body part acts on only one side of the body.

Language Development

Messy play increases language development because the nature of the materials encourages conversation. Children experience many tactile sensations when they play with slime, playdough, or other sensory materials, and they naturally want to describe those sensations verbally. Open-ended messy-play materials also lend themselves easily to dramatic play and all the conversations that result from this activity. For instance, children might build sand castles or clay "action figures" and create stories using these objects.

Cognitive Development

As mentioned earlier, messy play provides multisensory experiences that enhance cognitive development. Memories are most potent when they involve multiple sensory systems. For instance, if a child engages in dramatic play with grape-scented purple playdough, the rich sensory experience (including sound, scent, color, and texture) will engrain those memories more deeply into her mind. In short, information is easier to retrieve and retain when children learn it through multisensory experiences.

Messy play also allows a child to compare and contrast many different characteristics of sensory experiences. For example, a child can learn to distinguish between hot and cold and between soft and hard.

Social and Emotional Development

Many children calm themselves or learn to self-regulate through messy play. For instance, children who have a hard time calming down after an argument can use modeling clay to "knead out" their frustrations. Children with high levels of anxiety can also express nervous energy through this type of play.

The Cognition of Play

Teachers and family members often resist play-based preschool classrooms because they feel that children will miss out on learning essential academic skills and spend their time wearing dress-up clothes instead. Both teachers and families need to recognize that cognitive development occurs just as much during play as during any other activity in the preschool classroom. The following list describes some of the preacademic skills that children learn through play:

- When children draw pictures in the art area, they learn that symbols represent their ideas—a major precursor to reading and writing.
- When children put on and take off dress-up clothes, they strengthen their fine motor skills, especially the pincer grasp, which is essential for eventually learning to hold a pencil and write.
- When children play together in the dress-up area, they usually create a plot for their story. Learning to create a story with a beginning, middle, and end is a key skill for beginning reading and writing. Putting items in order (seriation) is also a key mathematical skill.
- When children mix two colors of paint or playdough to create a new color, they learn about cause and effect. Understanding this concept will aid children in learning about mathematical operations.
- When children use building blocks, they begin to match, sort, and classify—important mathematical skills—by shape, thickness, and size.
- When children play with blocks, they develop engineering, scientific-reasoning, and problem-solving skills. Working with different types and sizes of blocks can also improve visual memory.

Play can appear frivolous simply because children enjoy it so much, as many adults have been trained to believe that work and learning do not include enjoyment. However, as we have just seen, happily playing children actually learn many different skills. This type of play also teaches children to enjoy coming to school and learning. Such enthusiasm makes it much easier for teachers to encourage children to engage in challenging new experiences. Play also allows teachers to introduce new skills to children, because in play, the thrill of exploration often outweighs the stress of possible failure.

How Play Benefits the Whole Family

Play-based learning environments benefit not only young children but also their whole families. First, children in play-based classrooms (as opposed to classrooms where children mostly sit at desks) show more signs of being healthy and happy in the classroom. Preschoolers need to move their bodies frequently, and a classroom that allows for that movement also helps to create an interactive environment. Children who actively participate in engaging activities at preschool are eager to attend, separate more easily from family members, and want to tell their families all about their experiences at the end of the day. When children are happy at preschool, their family members can go to work and focus on their jobs without hesitation.

Children who play in group settings learn how to share, negotiate, and solve problems. They can also more easily initiate new friendships and try new things. These children can better handle the changes that a typical family experiences, such as moving, changing schools, or losing loved ones.

Encouraging Play at Home

Family members often wonder how to incorporate more play into their children's routines outside the classroom. Most families have such busy schedules that they have trouble setting aside large blocks of time for creating and imagining in the evenings and on the weekends. Encourage families not to overschedule their children's calendars. Children will have plenty of time for sports, dance classes, and so on in elementary school, but during preschool, they need unstructured time to learn and grow.

Even if families spend a lot of time away from their homes, they still have many ways to incorporate play into daily life. Early childhood educators can encourage family members to use activities such as the following to increase the amount of playtime they have with their children:

- Play simple games in the car, such as I Spy or finding pictures in the clouds.
- Cook together. This messy-play opportunity also allows children to practice math skills such as measuring and fine motor skills such as pouring and stirring.
- Along with or instead of reading picture books at bedtime, family members can take turns creating short stories.
- Find ways to turn daily chores into games, such as matching socks by color or jumping into piles of leaves before bagging them up.
- Turn grocery shopping into a scavenger hunt. Instead of going straight to the correct aisles, have children offer ideas about where to look for certain products.
- Enjoy some water play during bath time. Place measuring cups and spoons in the tub to help children learn about size and volume.
- Build a blanket fort in the living room, or have a picnic on the kitchen floor.
- Sing songs and dance together. Find or create unique songs that can help with daily routines, such as brushing teeth, getting dressed, or making beds.

Play, Emergent Curriculum, and School Readiness

Families frequently ask teachers for advice on how to practice literacy and numeracy at home, often expecting to receive recommendations for workbooks. However, preschoolers do not need to sit down and practice writing letters or numbers on worksheets; they need more time for experiential learning through play. When children are encouraged to play at school and at home, play becomes a regular part of their lives, and their play skills increase dramatically. To provide that consistent encouragement, teachers may need to offer families play suggestions in regular newsletters or through a classroom website or social-media page. Continued communication from teachers can help explain to families why adding more play to their days is the most important way to prepare their children for school.

The key idea to express to families is that children can prepare for school at home without completing worksheets. Families should focus on having interactive conversations with children and, at times, on helping children make their creativity tangible. For example, a mother can have a back-and-forth conversation with her child in the car about why the child enjoys living in a place with cold winters and what things the child enjoys that happen in cold weather. A father can ask his child to count the geese flying over their car while it sits at a stop sign. A grandmother can help her granddaughter design a pillow fort in the living room and then help the granddaughter problem solve to discover why the right side of the fort keeps falling down and how to fix it. All of these interactions address school-readiness skills, and children are more likely to participate in a conversation or playtime experience than they are to sit down at a table and do a worksheet after a long day of playing and learning at school.

chapter 4

"We Already Have a Curriculum"

Many, if not most, early childhood programs follow a published curriculum to guide teachers in lesson planning. Some educators assume that if they use such a curriculum, emergent curriculum is unnecessary ("I already know what I need to teach; it's all here in the manual.") or contradictory ("My boss says I have to use these units, but emergent curriculum says to let the children choose what they learn about. I can't do both."). Many high-quality curricula are, in fact, based on an emergent-curriculum framework. Furthermore, emergent curriculum can fit into any curriculum you might already use. This chapter explores how, using several popular curricula as examples.

Using Emergent Curriculum with HighScope

The HighScope curriculum focuses on strengthening all of children's major developmental areas, including cognition, language, social-emotional skills, and physical development. The design of the HighScope classroom allows children to construct their own learning by using materials in which they show interest. Teachers observe those interests so that they can create daily lessons focused on the children's strengths and can structure the environment in a way that motivates students to learn essential skills.

Using Emergent Curriculum with Montessori

Much like emergent curriculum, the Montessori preschool curriculum emphasizes observing children and individually addressing their curriculum needs. Montessori classrooms can plan in-depth projects that interest the students, but they also always provide materials that are not related to a theme. Granted, Montessori materials differ widely from those in a traditional play-based preschool classroom; however, Montessori teachers introduce materials to children based on their observations of the students' skill mastery and interest in new areas of learning.

For example, a Montessori classroom begins covering geography early in the preschool curriculum. The teacher might start by introducing the differences among land, air, and water and then move on to simple maps. If a three- or four-year-old child shows sincere interest in geography, he can then begin learning from maps of continents and countries. The teacher simply follows the child's interests and builds on the developmental skills that he has already mastered.

Using Emergent Curriculum with *The Creative Curriculum for Preschool* and *TeachingStrategies GOLD*

Many early childhood programs use *The Creative Curriculum for Preschool* (hereafter simply *The Creative Curriculum*) as their primary curriculum guide and *TeachingStrategies GOLD* as their curriculum-based assessment. *The Creative Curriculum* is a research-based early childhood curriculum that focuses on classroom exploration, social interactions, and critical thinking. The curriculum has thirty-eight specific learning objectives that involve teaching children school-readiness skills, from interacting with peers to classifying objects to maintaining balance while seated in a chair. *Teaching Strategies GOLD* is a curriculum-based assessment that partners with *The Creative Curriculum* to assess each child's progress in the classroom. This assessment also works with families to share developmental goals.

Emergent curriculum makes a wonderful complement to both *The Creative Curriculum* and *Teaching Strategies GOLD*. Let's examine how these three tools can work together.

The Creative Curriculum and Emergent Curriculum

Similarities

The Creative Curriculum and emergent curriculum have many similar goals. Both value a hands-on approach to learning in which children can freely explore the classroom environment while developing curiosity and problem-solving skills. Each curriculum promotes free-choice time and small-group learning experiences. Importantly, both systems encourage learning that focuses on investigating topics that the children find meaningful. Both curricula use a highly intentional approach to designing the environment, planning learning activities, and challenging each student.

The similarities between emergent curriculum and *The Creative Curriculum* also affect the adults involved in a preschool. Both tools focus on helping teachers to ask more open-ended questions of children and to use language development as a primary teaching tool in the classroom. Each curriculum attempts to find ways to include family members in the learning experience, either by inviting them into the classroom or by sending home communications to update them on children's learning.

Differences

Some aspects of *The Creative Curriculum* are more prescriptive than is usual in emergent curriculum. For instance, *The Creative Curriculum* directs teachers to use certain daily small-group activities and a "Question of the Day." However, as long as you do not plan too far ahead, you can easily incorporate these components into an emergent-curriculum program. For instance, if you plan a week in advance instead of a month in advance, you will have a much easier time making the "Question of the Day" and the daily small-group activities relevant to your students' current needs and interests.

Emergent curriculum adds a few components to the learning process beyond what *The Creative Curriculum* outlines in its essentials. Emergent curriculum requires attention to the aesthetics of the classroom. Because the classroom focus should be on the children's learning experience, the classroom is set up to prevent the children from being distracted by outside stimuli, such as too many decorations hanging from the ceiling.

Compared to *The Creative Curriculum*, emergent curriculum puts a greater focus on creation and loose parts by devoting part of the classroom to a laboratory or experiment area. Perhaps the largest difference between the two curricula is that emergent curriculum strongly discourages teachers from planning lessons too far in advance. Because children's interests change so often, this practice makes sure that teachers can incorporate the children's current interests into lessons, which helps the children stay engaged. *The Creative Curriculum*, on the other hand, does not specify how far in advance a teacher should plan.

TeachingStrategies GOLD and Emergent Curriculum

TeachingStrategies GOLD works well with emergent curriculum because teachers who use *TeachingStrategies GOLD* must continuously document the skills that the children learn in the classroom. The preschool version of this tool lists thirty-eight skills that children should learn in the classroom setting. These goals provide great benchmarks for emergent-curriculum teachers, helping them design activities to teach developmental skills. Additionally, both *TeachingStrategies GOLD* and emergent curriculum assess children's level of skill development and use the results to plan upcoming lessons and activities.

Combining *The Creative Curriculum*, *TeachingStrategies GOLD*, and Emergent Curriculum

Despite the differences among *The Creative Curriculum*, *TeachingStrategies GOLD*, and emergent curriculum, a teacher can easily combine them to promote successful outcomes for students. In a program that uses all three tools, the teacher observes the children, uses *TeachingStrategies GOLD* to determine their current level of mastery for each *Creative Curriculum* skill, and then plans activities that match the children's developmental levels.

The keys are to rely on the data from *TeachingStrategies GOLD* and to plan only a short time in advance so that you use the data in real time (or nearly so). You will still focus on the learning objectives from *The Creative Curriculum*, but you will teach them using content topics that interest the children, changing those topics as the children's interests change. You might even choose to use the overall lesson-plan format from *The Creative Curriculum*, including teaching its prescribed small-group lessons. That is fine. But always remember to pay attention to the children's questions and conversations during the day and to provide a variety of open-ended materials throughout your classroom.

chapter 5

Training Teachers in Emergent Curriculum

Many teachers go into the field of early education with detailed visions for their classrooms. Classroom decorations and displays often express teachers' thoughts and feelings, much as teachers' homes do. Teachers spend hours choosing topics and creating lesson plans based on subjects that interest them. If you, as a director, walk into a teacher's classroom and ask her to change how she teaches, she may feel as though you have attacked her very identity. You must handle this conversation delicately. Crucially, you need to show the teacher why she should change her methods and what benefits that change will bring.

It takes a specific type of educator to implement emergent curriculum successfully in the classroom. At a foundational level, teachers must willingly give up a certain level of control (as opposed to planning each part of each lesson) and open themselves to learning from their students. This can feel deeply unsettling, especially for teachers whose training tells them to plan far in advance and cover a certain list of thematic units each year. But ultimately, most early childhood educators work in this field because they want the best for the children they teach, so once they understand what children gain from emergent curriculum, these teachers will likely embrace it. This chapter explores how to help teachers move through this process.

Explaining the Benefits of Emergent Curriculum

Like anyone, teachers hesitate to change the way they do things unless they understand what they will gain from the alteration. Their lack of exposure to or experience with emergent curriculum can make them even more reluctant—what if the new way is no better or even worse than what they currently do? To overcome these reservations when discussing emergent curriculum with teachers, focus on two primary themes: how emergent curriculum benefits children and how it benefits teachers.

Benefits for Children	Benefits for Teachers
• Children develop intrinsic motivation for learning and enjoy coming to school. • Children feel empowered and realize that they can learn about things that interest them. • Children receive support to reach individualized developmental goals, as lesson plans reflect the needs of the current group of students. • Children can enjoy the act of learning because teachers do not pressure them to create a certain end product.	• Teachers do not waste their time making preproduced materials that do not interest or benefit the children. • Teachers have fewer behavior problems to deal with, so they can spend more time interacting with children. • Teachers can explore topics with the students and continue to be lifelong learners. • Teachers do not have to repeatedly use lesson plans that cause them to fall into a rut. • Teachers can incorporate child assessments into classroom activities instead of taking home additional work.

Motivating Experienced Teachers to Follow the Child

Understandably, experienced teachers may resist changing teaching methods that have worked well for them for years. Use the information in chapter 2 to ease these teachers' concerns by debunking common myths about emergent curriculum. However, you cannot stop there. The following additional activities may help veteran teachers open up to trying emergent curriculum:

1. Observing in a child-led classroom
2. Witnessing your support for a new program
3. Receiving communication and training from administrators
4. Hearing you acknowledge individual teachers' strengths
5. Witnessing support from children's family members

Arrange for Teachers to Observe

Any director can tell a dedicated teacher that the myths about emergent curriculum are incorrect. But if that teacher can observe in a successful emergent-curriculum classroom for a day, she receives concrete proof of what this method can do for teachers and children. Sending a teacher to an observation may cause you some difficulty, as you will have to juggle staff and schedules to make sure that all classrooms have the required ratios of teachers to children while that teacher is out. But these experiences are some of the most powerful ways to convince a teacher that a new technique is not only possible but also worth trying.

To arrange these observations, find a program or classroom that already uses a child-led curriculum, and develop a relationship with the staff there so that your staff members can occasionally observe in the classroom for a full day. A full day of observation allows the teacher to observe not only free-choice time but also many essential routines, such as meals, toileting, rest time, and transitions. These are key focus areas when changing a program from a preset curriculum to an emergent one.

Show Your Dedication to Emergent Curriculum

If you are a director who wants to implement emergent curriculum in your program, you must commit to the process. Such major changes require a top-down approach so that all classrooms make the necessary changes together. This approach also helps you better assist your experienced staff with training, materials, and general support as they attempt to change years- or decades-old practices and habits.

During this transition, teachers need your presence in the classroom more often than you might be accustomed to. Participate in child-led activities to provide models for teachers. Drop in to support teachers when they implement new lesson plans. Observe classrooms often so you can provide essential feedback when teachers have questions. Without your support and persistence, large-scale changes will not occur in your program.

Communicate and Train Early and Often

Communication and training are essential parts of any program transition. Training in emergent curriculum needs to begin well before you expect teachers to fully make the shift. Once the teachers have received the training they need, set up a reasonable timeline for system changes and spell out your expectations for the teachers. They need to understand the steps of the transition and the reasoning behind those changes so that they can willingly and effectively participate.

Family members will likely have questions about the transition to emergent curriculum and what it means for them and their children. As part of your regular communications with families, include information about what changes they should expect to see in the classrooms. Teachers will need to focus on their own change-related responsibilities, so encourage families to direct all questions about emergent curriculum to you or other administrators.

Change One Step at a Time

How would you feel if you came into your office one morning and found your furniture rearranged, saw new decorations on the walls, and discovered a note stating that effective immediately, you were to adopt a philosophy of administration that you had never heard of but that was detailed in the five-hundred-page handbook you found on your desk? You might quit on the spot! Similarly, when transitioning to using emergent curriculum, if you try to change every aspect of teachers' jobs at one time, you can overwhelm your staff. Instead, identify specific steps to help the teachers implement the necessary changes.

For example, if you want teachers to begin creating child-led lesson plans that focus on the interests and developmental needs of the children in their classrooms, you might break down that process into the following steps:

1. Introduce, or have another administrator introduce, a curriculum-based assessment, such as *TeachingStrategies GOLD*, and show teachers how to use it to track each child's individual development.
2. Lead or arrange for training sessions to show teachers how to use the data from your curriculum-based assessment to plan activities that address the various developmental levels of the children in their classrooms.
3. Model observation skills in the classroom, and show teachers how to learn about individual and group interests among the children.
4. Hold one-on-one conferences with teachers to further discuss how to write lesson plans based on developmental milestones and child interests.
5. Plan a staff meeting devoted to lesson-plan timelines to create the lessons as close to the time of implementation as possible. Teachers need to understand that, contrary to what they may be used to, they do not plan weeks and months in advance when implementing emergent curriculum.

This timeline may take six months to a year to implement in a program that currently uses something other than emergent curriculum. While that seems like a long time, it is possible. The keys are to communicate with teachers and to keep timelines realistic by not attempting to change the entire curriculum overnight.

 ## Case Study: Jessica Becomes an Emergent-Curriculum Convert

One of my friends, whom I will call Jessica, started her career at a church-based child-care center that used theme-based units. She first heard about emergent curriculum when she took a job with Bright Horizons, which required its teachers to use this method. Jessica received some initial training, but when she began teaching, she quickly realized that she still had no idea how to use emergent curriculum. For the first two months, she went home crying every day, and she spent weeks questioning the philosophy of this approach. But then, one day, the children changed her mind.

One of Jessica's students, whom I will call Tameron, was obsessed with robots. He came to school each day talking about the details of making robots and how they work. He even used the loose parts in the art area to create a full-sized robot. Within two weeks, the entire class had become interested in robots, and Jessica and the children ended up spending a whole unit studying them. Once Jessica saw the children's enthusiasm for learning about a topic that they had chosen, she knew she could never go back to planning the entire curriculum on her own. She has embraced emergent curriculum ever since.

Celebrate Successes

A large-scale change, such as implementing emergent curriculum, may cause teachers to question whether or not they were previously instructing the children well ("If what we did was fine, why are we changing?"), so they may feel insecure from the start. They also have to learn and implement multiple new skills. That process makes even the most confident teacher doubt herself at times, and during the transition, all the teachers become students again. They are learning a new way to be teachers, and it can feel as if someone is tinkering with the very core of who they are. Who *wouldn't* feel at least a little nervous?

Teachers need constant encouragement and support from all administrators during this time. Many leaders offer teachers generic praise (for example, "You're doing a great job!") throughout the day, but many teachers find such compliments hollow. Just as you train teachers to do with children, offer specific praise as soon as you see something positive. When teachers receive factual, immediate feedback, they can recognize what skills they have mastered and feel a specific pride with their actions. The following compliments provide some good examples:

- "I enjoyed watching you help Sam look up the answer to his question."
- "You've worked hard to allow the children to pass their own dishes at lunch time."
- "I've watched you use open-ended questions with all the children in your classroom. Thank you for making that change."

Sometimes administrators offer praise as if checking an item off a to-do list. Avoid doing this—teachers can identify insincere compliments and may resent you for giving them. Furthermore, make sure that you find ways to offer praise that relates to a teacher's meeting of established expectations. Making up a compliment does not help teachers understand their jobs. In fact, it can easily skew their interpretation of what you want from them or what their priorities should be. The things you praise are the things you get more of. For instance, if you tell Callie, "I love seeing your smile when you work with the children," she might understandably interpret that compliment as, "Smiling is important. I want you to keep doing that." Smiling does help create a welcoming classroom environment, but this is probably not the area where Callie should focus most of her attention.

Of course, it is important to develop a relationship with each staff member. You can and should have casual conversations with your staff and make sincere comments such as, "I love that outfit you have on today." During mentoring conversations, though, give specific praise that focuses on skills that you have seen the person demonstrate effectively in the classroom.

For teachers to feel successful in the classroom, they need positive feedback from two separate sources: administrators and families. Administrators need to communicate with families about teachers' hard work so families know what happens in the classroom. Celebrate staff members in ways that families can see. Many programs choose an employee of the month or give awards to individual staff members. Both honors are great ideas, but they celebrate only one person at a time. Instead, find visible ways to celebrate your staff as a whole. Try some of the following ideas:

- Use bulletin boards or social-media pages to post pictures of teachers doing special activities in their classrooms. The pictures can show individuals or teaching teams, but make sure to include teachers from across the program. **Note:** Before posting a photo anywhere (including on a bulletin board), obtain written permission from all the people in it. If the photo includes children, you must get written permission from their families.
- Use weekly or monthly newsletters to praise various teachers for their individual talents.
- Use classroom bulletin boards to show family members the skills that the teachers are helping their children learn. For instance, you might put up a sign that says, "Look what I'm learning!" followed by bullet points listing skills taught in the classroom, such as "Drinking from an open cup" or "Serving myself lunch." Many family members do not know that their children have certain skills, as the children do not use them at home. When families learn this exciting information, they often thank the teachers.
- When families plan activities for a teacher-appreciation event, encourage them to focus on the whole staff instead of on individuals so that all teachers receive expressions of gratitude.

Many educators stay in early care and education for years because of the encouragement and support they receive from colleagues, peers, and supervisors. When teachers feel respected and appreciated, it makes their jobs worthwhile. If teachers can see the impact they have on children and their families, they go home feeling accomplished. When teachers become discouraged, remind them about the power of their relationships with their students and families. They are the greatest reward of this field. Most teachers devote their lives to the field of education out of a desire to make a difference in the lives of children. On a rough day, strengthen their motivation by focusing their attention on the positive differences they have made.

Training New Teachers to Follow the Child

Although new early childhood teachers may not have much experience working with young children, they often come to your program willing to learn. That in itself can be a huge asset to any preschool. New teachers have typically not spent enough time in the field to develop bad habits or concrete job expectations, so you can more easily train them to use emergent curriculum and meet your program's specific expectations. This training is crucial because if staff members do not feel that they have the skills to do their jobs, they are much more likely to leave for jobs in which they can feel more successful.

The training process involves the following elements:

- State-mandated training
- Classroom observation
- Mentoring
- Real-time feedback
- Stay interviews (which we define later in this chapter)

State-Mandated Training

Every US state requires specific training for the staffs and administrators of child-care programs and preschools. Topics include health and safety requirements and how to identify child abuse. Staff members undergo mandatory background checks before they can begin working with young children. To comply with laws and regulations, always start new-teacher training with these essentials and keep all required records up to date.

Classroom Observations

Once new teachers have completed state-mandated training, have them observe in different classroom settings. This ideally happens in the first week or two of employment, though that may not work if you have a bare-bones staff. However, do your best to schedule those observations within the first three months of employment. Observing allows the new teacher to pick up ideas from different staff members and introduces her to the emergent-curriculum process.

If possible, have new teachers observe classrooms with children of various ages. Observing each age level allows new teachers to see the developmental continuum of the program and all that the children achieve while enrolled there. Because children develop at different rates, these observations can also give teachers ideas of how to work with children who develop faster or slower than most of their classmates. Even if, for example, a new teacher will work in a preschool classroom, it can be helpful to have her observe a kindergarten classroom so she can find potential activities for a preschooler with advanced skills. This chance to observe in multiple settings also allows the new teachers to meet their colleagues and start forming relationships.

Mentoring

After a new teacher has completed orientation and become somewhat acclimated to your program, assign another teacher to mentor and assist the new employee as she learns skills and discovers more about the program and about the classroom in which she will be teaching. The mentor need not have decades of experience, but she should exemplify the program's philosophies in her classroom. Although mentoring takes a lot of time and energy, many teachers are flattered to have this title and collaborate with their program directors to make sure they (the mentors) do a good job. Mentoring also offers an excellent opportunity for a teacher who would like to eventually move to an administrative role.

You and mentors need to work together to determine what the mentors will teach the new employees. One-on-one teaching from a mentor about, for example, assessment, lesson planning, or family-style dining often works better than having a teacher attend multiple group trainings on the same topics. Still, mentors should not be responsible for all of a new employee's program-specific training. You and your administrative team need to develop relationships with all new staff members, especially so the newcomers feel comfortable bringing questions or concerns to you. The exact division of training topics between mentors and administrators should primarily correspond to each party's skill set and level of comfort with topics. You and other administrators may want to take the responsibility for any training that specifically applies to job expectations or performance reviews, as you will be the ones monitoring these matters.

Feedback

As new employees begin to take on additional responsibilities, such as leading small-group activities for the first time or writing their first lesson plans, give them feedback in real time. For instance, you watch Lamesha lead a lesson, and you enjoy the warm, playful interactions she has with the children. When you give her this feedback, Lamesha is much more likely to repeat those types of interactions if she can remember what happened and what she did during that lesson. This means that the sooner you can give teachers feedback, the better. Waiting for an annual performance evaluation does not help shape a growing teacher. Rather, by the end of her first year, a teacher has formed habits and begun to develop her own sense of style, both of which might or might not mesh with your program. Instead, you and the teacher should have a constant conversation throughout the working year about what skills she is still developing and which ones she has mastered. (We talk more about performance evaluations later in this chapter.)

Many administrators worry about the balance between the positive and negative feedback that they give to their employees. Of course, no employee excels if she constantly receives negative feedback. You need to offer both positive and negative comments to truly benefit teachers. But instead of focusing on what percentage of your feedback is positive and what percentage is negative, consider the manner in which you give feedback.

Work to build a company culture that allows everyone, including teachers, mentors, and administrators, to make mistakes. Employees need to feel comfortable admitting to their errors without fear of retribution. Tell employees this on their first day, and stress it throughout the mentoring process. Mistakes are a part of life. Staff members should own up to them and find ways to prevent them from happening in the future. Choose mentors who demonstrate these habits; if a respected mentor acknowledges her own flaws, a novice teacher will also more likely admit to her mistakes.

Once an employee feels comfortable admitting mistakes, you can build a relationship with her that incorporates casual feedback. Feedback does not need to come from behind an intimidating desk. You can and should offer it in the same way you would handle a casual conversation. During these discussions, make sure to listen to the teacher's concerns and keep the focus on her instead of jumping in with your own stories. Use open-ended questions and statements to help the teacher brainstorm and work through situations.

When giving any kind of feedback, make it as sincere and authentic as possible. Honest communication, though it may initially feel awkward, will earn your teachers' respect and help them understand your expectations. Insincerity, on the other hand, makes it difficult for teachers (or anyone) to accept feedback. Why should they trust you if you are not honest with them?

 ## Case Study: Reviewing an Incident with Wendy

Germain, a preschool director, is observing in the classroom of four-year-olds taught by Wendy, a new teacher. A squabble breaks out between Isaac and Emily, who want to use the same small mat in the gross motor area. Wendy hesitates to intervene, and Emily suddenly pushes Isaac so hard that he falls onto the bare floor and has the wind knocked out of him. The loud noise and the sight of Isaac gasping on the ground frighten the other children, some of whom begin to cry or yell.

Germain steps in to help Wendy secure medical attention for Isaac, restore order, and properly document and report the incident. Thankfully, Isaac is not seriously hurt. After the children have left for the evening, Germain says to Wendy, "What a day, right? Tell me about Emily and Isaac. What do you think happened there?"

Wendy sighs. "I feel awful. I wasn't sure what to do, because I know we're supposed to let the children try to work through their own disagreements. But it escalated so quickly."

Germain nods. "Talking it out is a fairly new skill for children in this age group, so when they get upset, they tend to forget what they should do. What could you do to keep the next argument from escalating?"

Wendy thinks for a moment. "Well, I could go over to the children right away and . . ."

Performance Evaluations

If you have an ongoing dialogue with mentors and new teachers about performance and feedback, performance evaluations should not intimidate new teachers. These events simply become times to set authentic goals for the upcoming year. Because you have provided regular feedback to the teacher, you should not have to tell her, "This is what you are struggling with, and you should find ways to improve it this year." Instead, you can place the responsibility on her to find new ways to grow. This practice works well for both of you. It frees you from having to make certain decisions for the teacher, and she will likely have stronger motivation to pursue goals that she sets herself.

Stay Interviews

Many businesses use exit interviews to gather information from employees who leave for other jobs. A *stay interview* collects that same type of information from an employee, new or experienced, who stays with the company. You can use this time to check in with an employee to see whether she is happy in her position, whether she wants to stay in that position or earn a promotion, whether she would like to learn new skills or otherwise advance in her career, or whether she needs more support from management to do her job to the best of her ability. In this type of interview, give your full attention to the employee, and accept her feedback about the quality of the program and the administration.

The information you gather in a stay interview can improve the overall health of your program and help the employee advance her career. This type of interview can also let you know if the employee has established a timeline for moving on to a new position or occupation. For instance, a teacher who is enrolled in college may tell you that she plans to stay at your program for three more semesters and then leave when she earns her degree. This can help you create a timeline for training a replacement teacher and acclimating that person to the classroom.

When Teachers Leave

Despite your best efforts to give your teachers a solid foundation of training, there will always be some employees who figure out that they do not fit into your program. Not all employee loss is bad. When an employee realizes that she has little skill in or does not enjoy working with young children—even with extensive training, mentoring, and real-time feedback—that realization benefits both your program and her. No one wants to work in a job that makes her miserable, and a miserable teacher does little good for children, colleagues, or families. Losing this employee opens the door for you to hire a candidate who has greater passion for working with young children and who will support your preschool's vision.

You and others in your program will feel an emotional loss when a teacher resigns, because she has built relationships with you, other employees, children, and families. You may dread having to notify families about a staffing change, especially if they show frustration over the event. However, when a skilled teacher replaces the previous employee, the families will feel more at ease. They will develop new relationships with this teacher as they come to trust her.

chapter **6**

Explaining Emergent Curriculum to Families

If we look at early childhood education as a business, families are the consumers. When choosing a preschool, most families review the programs in their area and attempt to select the best option they can afford. They mainly look for a safe and loving environment where competent adults will care for and protect their children. Once families have found some programs that satisfy these basic requirements, they begin to look at secondary details, such as location, cost, accreditation, program reputation, and curriculum, including to what extent children learn school-readiness skills.

Many families want their children to be ready to start elementary school, but only some families accurately understand what skills a child needs to acquire before kindergarten. Family members frequently base their expectations for school readiness, and therefore for what a preschool will teach their child, on what they hear from friends and relatives who have older children. Family members also base their expectations on tuition costs. The higher the price, the bigger the return a family expects to receive on that investment.

Finding Out What Families Expect

Dialogue with families should begin as soon as family members reach out to your program to begin the application process. Preschools typically have marketing materials and family-member handbooks that they distribute to families who express interest in enrolling their child at that school. Families come to the preschool for a tour, and an administrator escorts them around the building to display the learning environment. He or another administrator explains the teacher-to-student ratio, the teachers' education levels, and the staff members' amount of experience. Family members use this information to make an informed choice for their children.

During the application process, the preschool should also collect information from prospective families. Of course, you will acquire much of this data from the paperwork, including facts such as a child's birthdate, his developmental history, and the family's contact information. You do need to keep this information on file, but as you give tours, you should also begin to find out what a given family expects from your preschool. Some families simply want a program that will keep their children safe while adult family members are at work. These families are typically thrilled when their children begin to acquire school-readiness skills. Other families may have specific lists of skills that they want their children to master and timetables for when they believe that mastery should occur.

Family members sometimes need help to form developmentally appropriate expectations for their children. This exercise benefits both preschools and children. When a family member expects a child to demonstrate skills that are not appropriate for his age (such as completing toilet training by age one), the family member can easily become frustrated with the child. In some cases, the family member even begins to punish the child for not using the desired skills. Similarly, when some family members enroll their child in preschool, they expect that their child will learn to write his name at age three or begin reading at age four, and they may become upset with the preschool if this does not happen. There will always be some children who develop more quickly than others, but family members need to understand typical developmental milestones so they can form reasonable expectations of what a child will learn in preschool. One of the best resources that teachers can refer families to for information about developmental milestones is the American Academy of Pediatrics (https://healthychildren.org/english/ages-stages/pages/default.aspx).

Educating Families about What Happens in the Classroom

Through education and experience, a preschool teacher obtains a wealth of knowledge about the abilities of young children. He needs to share this knowledge with family members. Whereas schools once conveyed this type of information to families primarily on paper, many programs have begun to use various media platforms to share such knowledge. Technology can provide an easy, convenient method for educating families, but some lessons are best taught face to face. For instance, if a teacher needs to share delicate information—such as observations about challenging behavior or about developmental skills that the child struggles with—it works best to sit down with the family to make sure that they understand the teacher's concerns and vice versa. Preschools must find a balance among all these forms of communication to serve families effectively. Let's explore some useful communication tools.

Open Houses

Many preschools hold open houses near the beginning of the school year to introduce family members to the schools' educational philosophies and developmental expectations for enrolled children. If you host an open house, request that children stay at home to minimize distractions. When a family member brings his children to school meetings, he often spends the entire meeting worrying about the children's behavior and does not get much, if any, of the information he came for.

Open house makes a great time to talk more about how emergent curriculum works in your program. Many family members look for tangible daily products as a concrete sign of the return on their investment in their children's education, so you need to explain that in an emergent-curriculum school, children do not bring home daily work. Help families understand that *what* the children create is not as important as *how* they create it. Many schools address this topic by talking about the scientific process of discovery. Families often want their children to start learning about math and science early, so when staff explain about teaching with open-ended questions and using the scientific method, many family members open up to the idea of fewer paper products.

An open house also lets family members explore classrooms and see what types of materials the children use each day. Family members can then ask the teachers about each material's role in the learning environment. This background knowledge benefits the children, because when a child comes home talking about classroom activities, his family members can identify what he means and can more easily participate in the discussion.

Family-Education Nights

Whereas open houses introduce families to the school as a whole, family-education nights focus on specific educational topics. For instance, one night might focus on how the program uses assessments for lesson planning. Another night might show how the teachers use the children's interests to select a theme for a child-led project. A third night could have family members move from room to room to learn about how teaching teams in the infant, toddler, three-year-old, and preschool classrooms plan their lessons. Still another night could include a panel discussion and question-and-answer session about emergent curriculum. Families need to understand that while teachers of the same age group typically teach the same developmental skills each year, the students in each class often select the lesson topics, which are the medium through which the children learn the needed skills.

Ideally, you should have two to three family-education nights throughout the course of the school year to help family members understand the school's curriculum and educational philosophy. If you have trouble deciding which topics to cover, examine the types of questions that families are asking the teachers and administrators. You can also select topics based on which subjects you have covered in the past several years and how many of the currently enrolled families have already heard about those topics. Beneficial topics for these activities include the following:

- Your program's assessment system and how families and teachers can communicate about results
- Skill- or topic-specific curricula used in your program, such as Handwriting without Tears
- The importance of routines and schedules
- How play-based fine motor activities build handwriting skills
- Social-emotional skills used in the preschool classroom
- What true school readiness looks like and why academic learning is only one piece of it
- Family-style dining
- The effects of language skills on early literacy
- Project-based learning

Resource Lists

Some family members always want to know more about what their children are learning and how to prepare them for school. When schools do not provide resources for these families, they typically turn to the internet for more information, and they may or may not find developmentally appropriate information about early childhood education. To avoid this confusion, schools should keep a list of resources that family members can go to, to find accurate information. This list should include information on topics such as the following:

- Child-development milestones
- Developmental delays
- Local pediatricians and early childhood specialists
- Emergent curriculum
- Project-based learning
- *TeachingStrategies GOLD* and/or other assessments used in your program

You can easily create this list by making a digital document with links to education-based websites that share accurate information about the selected topics. You can post the list on the preschool's website as a resource for all families, or you can make it private and only send the link to family members who individually approach staff with questions about child development or early learning. After completing the list, assign a staff member to check it regularly to update links and contact information as needed.

Improving Classroom Communication

Because children often spend more awake time each day with preschool teachers than with their own family members, preschools need to communicate with families about the overall learning in the classroom and a child's individual accomplishments. Teachers often share their weekly lesson plans and general goals for their entire classrooms, but when a child has a learning breakthrough, it is also important to share those exciting moments with his family. This can get tricky because in full-day preschool programs, family members may not be able to speak with the same teacher at both drop-off and pick-up time (we will see why in a moment). Therefore, staff members need a way to standardize and streamline communication among themselves and with families so that each family receives necessary information about their child's health, temperament, and achievements.

Ideally, in a preschool, the same teaching team works together every day and develops lesson plans together. They stagger their hours so that at least one teacher is present for morning drop-off time and at least one is present for evening pick-up time, but their shifts overlap in the middle of the day so that they can share information and teach essential lessons together. In this type of setting, the teachers know children's family members well and can communicate key daily information, including answers to common or family-specific questions (such as "We did X, Y, and Z today" or "You asked us to keep you updated about Felicia's language development. This morning, she . . .").

To make sure this teacher-to-family communication happens, teachers keep each other informed about important events that occur when one or more of them is not present. For instance, four-year-old Kwame learns to tie his shoe one morning. Teacher Vance gives him a celebratory high-five. When Julio, Vance's coteacher, arrives for his shift that afternoon, Vance tells him about this event. Now no matter which teacher sees Kwame's family at pick-up time tonight, that teacher can share the exciting news.

Remember, this is the ideal for teacher-to-teacher and teacher-to-family communication. Many different factors can affect how communication actually works at your preschool.

 Case Study: Common Obstacles to Communication

It is 7:30 a.m. at director Ofelia's preschool, and every common staffing difficulty seems to have occurred at once. Among the teachers, Nalani is on vacation, Xaviera has a doctor's appointment and will not arrive until 8:30, and now Quentin has called in sick. Ofelia begins making phone calls to find another substitute for the day.

Once she has secured a temporary staff member, Ofelia leaves her office to greet arriving families. Mrs. Baker drops off her daughter, Michelle, and then approaches Ofelia to ask about pick-up-time procedures. The program handbook states that families should normally direct these sorts of questions to teachers. However, an interim teacher named Erin took charge of Michelle's class just last week after another teacher suddenly resigned, and Ofelia knows that many family members do not yet feel comfortable approaching Erin. Ofelia easily answers Mrs. Baker's general questions but cannot provide specific details about something that happened yesterday afternoon in Michelle's classroom, as Ofelia was not present during the incident. She suggests that Mrs. Baker talk to Michelle's afternoon teacher, Vicki, who will arrive later in the day. Mrs. Baker agrees and leaves.

Back in her office, Ofelia sends an email to all her teachers and substitutes, even those not on duty today. With such confusing staffing arrangements for the day, now seems like a good time to remind everyone of the policies and procedures for sharing information among staff.

Ideas for Simplifying Communication

Because of events and complications such as the ones Ofelia encountered, the teaching staff need a plan in place to make teacher-to-teacher and teacher-to-family communication as simple as possible. The following list offers some ideas:

- Use daily transition notebooks, in which morning teaching teams can write notes for afternoon teaching teams to share with family members, and vice versa.
- Fill out daily sheets with two parts (morning and afternoon) for each child, and give them to family members at the end of the day.

- When many people need to receive the same information, send out mass text messages to families or teaching teams from an app such as Remind. Make sure to have permission from each person before contacting him in this way.

Some preschool programs now use software programs, such as Tadpoles, that allow staff members to use electronic daily sheets. A teacher fills in some information that applies to all children, such as the day's meals and lesson-plan activities, so the program can autopopulate those fields. Then the teacher can fill in personalized information for each child, such as adding individual photos and comments about a child's day. These forms go out to families by email at the end of the day, so even if the teacher who made a certain note has already left by pick-up time, family members can still receive all available daily information about their child. Administrators can also use Tadpoles to send larger-scale reminders, such as "Picture day is tomorrow," to all families.

TeachingStrategies GOLD uses similar technology. Assessment results "live" online so that family members can log in and see their children's records. Teachers can use the online system to message family members. They can also upload photos to document a child's development, activities, and progress in learning various skills. When family members see these pictures, they feel more secure about the quality of the care that their child receives, even though they cannot witness it in person.

Some preschools install video cameras and give family members access to a live feed so they can log in during the day and view what happens in their children's classroom. This system of communication can have both positive and negative effects. The high level of transparency can definitely give family members peace of mind. However, this type of system raises significant privacy concerns. Some families simply do not like the idea of strangers watching their children over the internet. A family whose child has a disability or medical condition might not want other families to know that the child receives special-education services or prescribed treatments in the classroom. Cameras can also make it tricky to maintain privacy during diapering and toileting.

Another drawback of a live-video system is that it rarely shows everything. A camera is typically placed where it can capture the widest field of view, but that field often does not cover the entire classroom. If something occurs at the edges of the camera's field of view, viewers can easily misinterpret actions. Even if a concerning incident happens in full view of the camera, grainy images can raise doubts about a teacher's or a child's actual behavior.

Consider both pros and cons before you install classroom cameras, start live feeds, or both. Even if you do not share the actual videos with families, you can use still images taken from those videos to illustrate for family members what their child's day was like.

Holding Effective Parent-Teacher Conferences

Parent-teacher conferences provide a high-quality way of establishing communication between families and teaching teams. It can benefit both families and teachers to dedicate time to sitting down and discussing a child's development. Teachers can share information about what the child does at school and how his skills are growing. Family members, the true experts on a child, can provide valuable details about what the child likes and what strategies the family uses at home for learning and for managing behavior.

Overcoming Family Members' Reluctance

Some family members dislike parent-teacher conferences because in their own childhoods, these conferences happened mainly when they got into trouble at school. As a result, these family members may believe that any request for a parent-teacher conference means that their child is in trouble, and if they come to the conference at all, they will likely have their defenses up from the moment they walk in the door.

Both teachers and family members need to see parent-teacher conferences as tools for learning, not discipline. Families need to experience the process of positive information sharing so they can feel that they and the teachers are on the same team, working together to benefit children. To this end, try offering regularly scheduled parent-teacher conferences two to three times a year. If everyone receives invitations to these conferences, family members are less likely to assume the worst about why you want to meet with them.

Scheduling

Although parent-teacher conferences have traditionally taken place face to face at strictly scheduled times in school buildings, today's teachers have some additional options for holding conferences:

- Visits at a child's home
- Conference calls
- Video calls

Remember to consider several factors when choosing a method for conference. If you offer one family an alternative to a face-to-face conference at the school, you need to make that option available for any family. If your school uses home visits, take safety precautions, such as going on each visit with a colleague and calling ahead to make sure that the family expects you at the appointed time. If you use a conference or video call, email any essential documents to the family in advance so that they can review them with you at the time of the conference. If these documents contain private or sensitive information, consult your program's electronic-communications policy *before* sending the email.

Choosing What to Discuss

Focus on Growth

No matter which meeting method you use, keep the conference focused on the child's developmental milestones and other growth. At a beginning-of-the-year conference, show the family the child's beginning-of-the-year assessment information, and discuss with them reasonable learning goals for the school year. At a midyear or end-of-the-year conference, the teacher should focus on the child's growth. Use the information from observations and assessments to show the family which skills the child has mastered or has begun to demonstrate since the beginning of the year. Discuss how the child spends his time in the classroom and what centers he enjoys the most. Encourage the family members to ask questions and share concerns.

Discuss Developmental Concerns Carefully

If assessment or observation data begin to show that a child is developing more slowly than expected, introduce that information sensitively. A beginning-of-the-year conference is typically not the best time for that discussion, because at this point, you have only collected baseline data and do not know the child or the family well yet. If you express concern about a child's development early in your relationship with the family, the family members may react defensively: "How dare you think there's something wrong with my child? You don't even know us!" Avoid this kind of tension by making sure to spend adequate time observing the child's learning process before you decide whether to speak to the family about seeking further help for him. Check with your administrators before contacting the family, and if your school has a procedure for introducing this type of information to a family, follow it. If your school staff includes specialists such as an early interventionist or a speech pathologist, seek information from those colleagues.

> Psychologist and researcher Ginger Welch's book *How Can I Help? A Teacher's Guide to Early Childhood Behavioral Health* provides a wonderful resource for recognizing symptoms of possible mental-, behavioral-, and developmental-health concerns in children. It also offers ideas for supporting these children and their families in the classroom and during the referral process.

On the other hand, if the family members pursue the topic of a developmental delay at a beginning-of-the-year conference, they have clearly identified an issue that you need to act on. Again, the family members are the experts on their child, so if they have a concern about his development, they will need your support and possibly a referral to other professionals to help the child get the assistance he needs. Encourage the family to start the evaluation process by speaking with the child's pediatrician for guidance. During this process, the doctor may ask for your observations about the child. Make sure to obtain the family's written permission first, but this exchange of information can be a helpful way for you to support the child.

Explain Assessment Tools and Methods

If your program uses a specific assessment tool, such as *TeachingStrategies GOLD*, take time at each conference to make sure that family members understand the tool and any related apps or support programs available for them. Also explain how else teachers in your program document children's learning. Preschool teachers typically use a list of developmental skills (such as those in *The Creative Curriculum*) to evaluate students over the course of the school year. The teacher might, for instance, document when the child begins attempting to use a certain skill and when he demonstrates mastery of the skill. The teacher can share this type of documentation with the child's family. If family members understand how staff track developmental milestones and plan new learning activities based on those milestones and the children's interests, the family members typically have fewer concerns about a lack of children's artwork and papers coming home.

For instance, family members often express worries similar to this one: "All my child does is come to school and play dress-up or paint. How is that going to help him get ready for kindergarten?" Prepare for these conversations by creating documents that break down the school-readiness skills that children learn in the dramatic-play, art, or block areas. Families typically show most concern about these areas, though you could prepare a document for each center in your classroom if desired. Once family members understand that their child *is* preparing for school as he plays, they will likely feel much better and accept that their child will not bring home as many papers or projects as they might expect.

Using Photo Documentation

Photo documentation is one of the best ways to show families what children accomplish in an emergent-curriculum classroom. Not only do family members love to see photos of their children, but in the absence of worksheets or crafts, photos also give family members a concrete understanding of what their children do during the school day.

You can use photo documentation in many different ways. The following list gives a few examples*:

- Display photo boards throughout the school or the classroom. Include pictures that show activities from various subject areas (for example, science experiments or math manipulatives) and live-action learning (such as large-group activities, dances, and meal times). You can use photos from one or more classrooms.
- Post daily or weekly updates about classroom activities on private, invitation-only blogs or social-media pages. Many families enjoy viewing classroom activities while at work or home.
- Teachers can send photos to individual family members through phone or tablet apps.
- Software programs designed for early education programs, such as Tadpoles, allow teachers to send personalized information directly to families, including daily and weekly updates.

When teachers use photo documentation, children can focus on learning and exploring rather than on completing a battery of sit-down assessments. In fact, photos can document development for assessments and for updates to family members. You can even compile photos of each child into a collection and present it to his family at the end of the year.

Your program must set its own policies and procedures for photo documentation. If teachers are permitted to use their personal phones or tablets to take photos, how will they transfer that documentation to school records and then remove it from their devices to protect children's privacy? To avoid having staff members get distracted by other uses of their personal devices, a preschool might require that teachers use only school cameras for photo documentation. In this case, the school will need to provide access to a camera for each classroom. But once your program has these technical details worked out, photo documentation can be a great asset to teachers and families.

*Note: Before posting a photo on a bulletin board, online, or anywhere else, make sure to obtain written permission from all the people in it. If the photo includes children, you must get written permission from their families.

chapter 7

Using Emergent Curriculum to Build School Readiness

The increasingly popular term *school readiness* is used by educators and families to describe a child's ability to succeed in kindergarten. Teacher-accountability and elementary-school standards have continued to increase. Five- and six-year-old kindergarteners are now expected to sit at desks for the majority of the school day and focus on what a teacher is saying for extended periods of time. Instead of exploring with hands-on learning, they work on literacy and math skills at their desks from the first day of school.

Because kindergarten expectations have become so daunting, the view of preschool education has drastically changed. If children need academic skills to succeed in kindergarten, many families want their children to begin learning those skills as early as possible. This often means that other important developmental objectives, such as learning social and motor skills, are pushed aside to devote more time to learning beginning literacy and numeracy.

Preschools now have challenging choices to make. Do they follow the practices promoted by child-development specialists for decades, or do they follow consumer demand to make sure that children can sit at desks and do seat work from the first day of kindergarten? Because many preschools are also small businesses, their owners may feel that they must follow their customers' requests. However, attempting to impose kindergarten-level demands in the preschool classroom does not guarantee the desired outcomes. In fact, placing unreasonable goals on young children may contribute to behavior problems and to children's developing negative views of school.

When asked, kindergarten teachers frequently explain that they have been trained to teach children the alphabet and help them learn to read. If students arrive at kindergarten without essential social skills (such as following directions, standing appropriately in a line, or playing well with others) or self-help skills (such as using the restroom independently or feeding themselves at lunch), teachers may have to delay academic learning to help the children acquire these competencies. Otherwise, their classrooms will likely become chaotic, and even if the teachers manage to teach any academic skills in these environments, they may not stick.

Based on this information, it appears that school-readiness skills include not just academic knowledge but also development in other areas. Teachers and families must understand basic patterns of development to accurately judge what a typical five- or six-year-old can do when she first enters the kindergarten classroom.

Building on Emergent Curriculum

The Foundation of School Readiness

Although many people define *school readiness* as "the quality of being prepared to begin the academic work of kindergarten," a more appropriate definition may be "the quality of being prepared to learn and be successful." In this light, describing a child as "ready for school" suggests that she can follow multiple-step directions, play well with other students, demonstrate curiosity to learn, and absorb the information that her teachers will present over the course of the school year. More specifically, school readiness includes six categories of habits, practices, and skills, as shown in the following table.

Health and Physical Development	• Gets adequate sleep • Gets proper nutrition • Receives needed immunizations and regular medical and dental care • Climbs, jumps, runs, and performs other gross-motor activities • Uses pencils, crayons, scissors, and paint and performs other fine motor activities
Language and Communication	• Speaks with children and adults • Takes turns in a conversation • Uses sentences of five to six words • Knows first and last name • Can recite home address, phone number, and birthday • Sings simple songs • Listens and responds to stories read to her • Reads and writes own name • Knows how a book works (written from front to back and from left to right) • Recognizes familiar print and symbols from surroundings (traffic signs, logos, and so on) and understands that these shapes mean something • Uses scribbles and drawings to express ideas • Recites the letters of the alphabet (even before knowing which sounds the letters make)

Social and Emotional Development	• Plays and shares with other children • Separates easily from family members • Works well alone • Demonstrates dramatic play • Expresses own needs and wants • Complies with simple routines and rules • Explores and tries new things • Focuses on one activity until it is complete • Asks for help when unable to solve a problem independently
Independence and Self-Regulation	• Uses the toilet without help • Feeds self with utensils • Fastens and unfastens clothing (zippers, snaps, Velcro) without help • Helps put away toys and clothing • Keeps track of personal belongings • Covers mouth and nose when sneezing or coughing • Washes hands with soap and water • Is enthusiastic about learning new things • Is curious about the world around her • Can calm down after becoming upset or angry • Can understand classroom rules and why everyone should follow them • Can express values that are important to her and her family
Cognitive and Preacademic Skills	• Can identify items that are the same and different • Classifies and sorts objects • Recognizes basic colors • Knows, identifies, and copies basic shapes • Counts by ones (rote counting) up to thirty • "Counts sets of objects up to ten" (Kentucky Governor's Office of Early Childhood) • Matches the printed number with objects up to ten (for example, matches the numeral 6 with six real coins) • Asks questions such as who, what, when, where, how, and why • Understands simple concepts of time (night, day, today, yesterday, tomorrow)

Sources: Center for Family Services; Kentucky Governor's Office of Early Childhood

Using this list, preschool teachers and families can establish reasonable goals for five-year-olds to achieve before starting kindergarten. For instance, an incoming kindergartener should be able to write her own name, as it is the most common word she will encounter during the school day. However, she is not developmentally ready to read a list of sight words and copy them correctly. If a student is advanced for her age, her teacher can and should help her learn additional skills. Still, the teacher should not expect this child to master a list of kindergarten skills before even beginning kindergarten. If the child could do that, why would she need to attend kindergarten instead of going straight to first grade?

Remember, each child learns and develops uniquely. Some children do not master many school-readiness skills prior to entering kindergarten. This delay can happen for many different reasons, including the following:

- The child might not yet have shown interest in certain skills. Once she joins a structured kindergarten classroom, she may acquire those skills. Many kindergarteners gain interest in literacy and numeracy activities once they are more mature or when they see the rest of their classmates participating in these types of activities.
- Children do not all learn at the same pace, so a child who lags behind her peer group may simply be learning on her own schedule. Each developmental skill has a window of time during which most children master that skill. For instance, in the article "Developmental Milestones: 4-to-5-Year-Olds," the American Academy of Pediatrics indicates that between ages four and five, a child learns how to get dressed and undressed independently. Some children master the skill at the beginning of the window, while others may take more time. If the child has still not mastered the skill once the typical window of time is complete, then the teacher may need to seek additional support.
- The child might have a developmental delay. The kindergarten teacher should observe the child in the classroom setting before deciding whether to refer the child for a developmental assessment. Environmental factors might be preventing her from demonstrating a skill that she actually can use. For example, a child may never come to the writing table because that area of the classroom is loud and she does not like that level of auditory stimulus. If the teacher finds such environmental factors, she can alter the environment to help the child master the skill. However, if your observations show that the child does try to demonstrate the skill but struggles to do so, it may be time to speak with her family to see whether the child demonstrates the skill at home or whether further evaluation should take place.

Let's explore each school-readiness category in more detail.

Health and Physical Development

Maintaining Health

After reading the list in the previous section, you may ask, "Why include health-promotion techniques on a list about school readiness?" These practices help prevent children from becoming sick so they can consistently attend school. The basic rule of school attendance, even from a young age, is that if a child misses school, she also misses learning the content from that day. The more daily content she misses, the farther behind her peers she will become. Healthful meals, regular doctor's appointments, adequate rest, and immunizations help prevent many childhood illnesses, enabling children to enjoy being healthy and attending school daily. Healthy development also strengthens all of the other developmental domains so that a child can build her entire skill set.

A child's family plays a crucial role in helping her develop the health and wellness skills and habits that will help her succeed in school. For example, to focus and learn each day, a child must get enough rest. This means that her family members need to set an appropriate bedtime, ensure that her environment promotes quality sleep (such as by keeping televisions and video-game systems out of bedrooms), and establish bedtime routines that help the child fall asleep easily each night. Similarly, because children do not yet know how to choose healthful foods, how to ward off disease, or when to see a doctor, families must also establish proper nutrition and regular doctor's appointments for their children. Pediatricians typically share this type of information with families, but teachers can provide reminders and tips. The overall goal of these health practices in preschool is to set the stage for continuing healthy development in elementary school and to make sure that a child's health does not limit her ability to learn.

Motor Skills

To hold a pencil and manipulate it well enough to write letters and numbers, a child must have well-developed fine motor skills. However, a child's muscles develop from the core of the body out toward the extremities, so before learning to write, she must first have strong gross motor skills. This means that she needs to learn to run, jump, climb, and skip not only to stay healthy but also to write her name. Many families judge their preschoolers' progress toward writing by observing whether their children bring home worksheets full of hand-printed letters. However, preschool teachers more commonly help children prepare to write by encouraging them to participate in activities that strengthen both large and small muscles, such as climbing playground equipment, playing with modeling clay, and painting large murals on an easel.

Language and Communication

Language skills have a huge effect on a child's social skills, including the ability to engage in conversation and extract new information from the environment around her. A key quality indicator for a preschool classroom is to what degree the classroom environment encourages language development. Some indicators in the physical classroom space, such as labels on the shelves for materials or an alphabet poster on the wall, show efforts to build language skills. However, we can only truly assess the amount of emphasis on language development by observing interactions between teachers and students throughout the school day.

First and foremost, to be ready for elementary school, children need to be able to use and understand words to communicate. A family member typically understands a child's speech sooner than anyone else can, but when the child goes to preschool, she has to communicate clearly with others who do not know her as well. For example, she needs to be able to tell a teacher if she needs to use the restroom, is upset, or does not feel well. Preschool also gives a child the opportunity to interact with a wide variety of non-family members. She must learn to use her language skills to get along with different types of people, convey information to them, and understand them when they talk to her.

As a child participates in many conversations with others, she acquires a larger vocabulary. This skill helps her communicate more details to others in conversation and, as discussed earlier in this book, begins to prepare her for reading. She can also use that larger vocabulary to learn more in-depth concepts and respond to questions. For example, when a teacher reads a book to a child and asks her a question about the text, the child will more likely be able to comprehend the story and put her thoughts into words if she has a large vocabulary to draw on. These language skills are not easy to document, but they are the foundation for initial reading skills and a key component of the early childhood classroom.

Social and Emotional Development, Independence, and Self-Regulation

We often use the terms *social skills* and *emotional skills* interchangeably, but they are two different sets of abilities, and independence and self-regulation play important roles in both sets.

- *Social skills* enable the child to follow the social rules of the classroom and school: walking in a line in the hallway, being quiet at appropriate times, keeping food on the table in the school lunchroom, and so on. Social skills also include the ability to get along with other children in a classroom setting. This can mean, for instance, sharing classroom materials or playing independently even when other students are present.

  » Every social environment (school, work, church, and so on) has social rules, and children should begin to learn these at a young age. For example, running is appropriate on a playground but not in a place of worship.

- *Emotional skills* enable a child to identify, manage, and express her emotions.

Self-Regulating

As a child grows, she needs to learn to identify the emotion or emotions she feels and process those emotions so that she understands how to act in a given situation without assistance from an adult. This skill is called *self-regulation*. As anyone who has witnessed a toddler's temper tantrum can attest, self-regulation takes time and practice to develop, especially when strong emotions overwhelm a child.

To help children develop self-regulation, preschool teachers frequently ask them to "use your words" to express their emotions. In her book *PUSH PAST It! A Positive Approach to Challenging Classroom Behaviors*, child-development specialist Angela Searcy points out that for children to be able to comply with this request, adults must teach them the words needed to describe feelings. Once a child can identify her current emotion, a teacher can offer suggestions on the best way to respond to that emotion in the classroom setting. As children grow, adults should teach more possible ways to express and manage emotions. For example, if a toddler feels sad, she will likely cry to deal with that emotion. As she gets older and develops other skills, she learns from the adults around her that crying is not the only thing she can do when she feels sad. She can, for instance, spend time alone or ask her teacher for help instead.

A kindergarten-ready child has enough self-regulation skill to identify and control her emotions during everyday activities. She can handle a small amount of frustration without a loud outburst and can calm down on her own. She can deal with minor daily changes and setbacks. Furthermore, her reactions are proportional to their stimuli. For example,

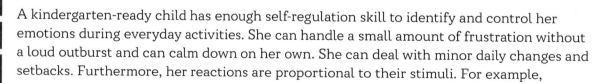

Building on Emergent Curriculum

if another child accidentally bumps into her, she does not respond by screaming or throwing things.

Developing self-regulation allows a child to focus her attention on the task at hand instead of becoming overly emotional about small, outside events. This may mean that if, say, a field trip is cancelled, the child might feel sad about it, but the event does not completely derail her behavior for the remainder of the day or week. On the other hand, if a preschooler or kindergartener suffers a traumatizing event, such as a death or divorce in her family, she will likely need assistance dealing with her emotions, just as an adult might need similar help.

Self-regulation plays an important part in the social rules of the classroom. To operate as a member of the class, a child must be able to communicate her wants and needs in a way that the rest of the group will understand. She must also understand that the classroom has certain behavior expectations, such as "use walking feet" or "use gentle hands," and control her own behavior to follow those rules. During group work, the child also learns to adjust her actions to comply with social rules that generally go unspoken. For example, if she gets too close to a classmate during a conversation, the classmate might tell her to scoot back or might even push her away. Through these experiences, the child learns how much personal space to give others.

Following Directions

Because kindergarten teachers frequently give directions and expect children to complete those instructions independently, children need to learn how to follow directions before starting kindergarten. This process involves mastering several skills. First, a child must learn how to listen to others and process their requests. She needs to comprehend not only words but also body language, facial expressions, and tone of voice. Second, once a child understands a request, she must remember essential information until she has completed the instructions. This skill improves with age. By age two or three, a child can follow one-step requests such as "Come here" or "Put the toy away." By the time a child starts kindergarten, she should be able to follow multiple-step directions.

Getting Along with Others

Although preschool classrooms may have small numbers of children, kindergarten classrooms can have as many as twenty-five to thirty students in the same room. Kindergarteners must share table space, materials, and the teacher's attention, perhaps more than they ever have had to before. If a child cannot interact well with other students, the teacher must devote a large amount of classroom time to mediating fights instead of teaching academics.

To help children learn to get along, teachers and families should provide many opportunities for children to play in groups. This is one of many reasons why preschool is so essential. Families can teach children about letters and numbers at home, but nothing can replace the hands-on learning that occurs when a child spends time in a group with other children.

When playing in groups, a child learns many important social and emotional skills. She uses problem solving to figure out how to work through disagreements by talking instead of hurting a playmate. She learns when she needs to step aside for a moment to collect her composure, and she discovers how to communicate that need to other children. The child also comes to understand that classroom materials belong to the group, not to an individual child, and she develops coping skills when she sees peers playing with toys that she also enjoys. She masters all these skills over time as she practices transitioning to new situations or interacting with new people.

Cognitive and Preacademic Skills

Preacademic skills are the abilities that many families think of when they hear the term *school readiness*. As families choose a preschool, they may ask teachers and administrators when children will learn these skills, hoping to verify that their child will be prepared to enter kindergarten the following year. Most preacademic skills fall into two categories: *preliteracy* (preparing children to read and write) and *prenumeracy* (preparing children to do math). Preliteracy includes exposing children to books, allowing the children to look at picture books and create a story, encouraging children to write invented letters or words, and identifying environmental print (pictures in the daily environment that have meaning, such as the symbol on a bathroom door in a store). Prenumeracy includes comparing same and different items, classifying objects, placing items in order, identifying shapes and colors, and starting to learn about the concepts of more and less. Along with mastery of preacademic skills must come curiosity to learn.

Literacy Skills	Numeracy Skills
• Familiarity with handling books • Letter recognition • Phonetic sound recognition (knowing what sounds each letter makes) • Writing	• Shape and color identification • Pattern and quantity identification • Number recognition • Rote counting (counting sequentially by ones) • One-to-one counting (counting one item at a time)

How Teachers Can Help

Preschool teachers should provide children access to literacy and numeracy materials in the classroom setting. For instance, teachers can place printed words around the classroom by labeling materials or posting classroom rules. A number line or a clock on the wall can provide numeracy displays. Children also need daily access to books. Teachers should read to individuals and groups, and children should have opportunities to explore books on their own.

Teachers can use simple conversations to introduce many preacademic skills. For example, a teacher may work numeracy concepts into a conversation by saying, "How many flowers do you see on the playground?", "Let's count how many blocks are in your tower," or "I see the red stop sign. How many sides does it have?" To weave in literacy concepts, she might say, "There's an *S* on that sign. What sound does *S* make?" When families and teachers bring literacy and numeracy concepts into typical conversations, children begin to learn these concepts more easily than they would when seated at a table doing a structured activity that might or might not interest them. Individual conversations and attention can have a powerful effect on children. Sometimes these factors stimulate additional learning simply because a child feels secure enough to explore, is happy to have an adult's attention, or wants to please the adult.

Teachers should also incorporate handwriting exploration into the classroom. Children should have daily access to blank paper and crayons, pencils, markers, and other writing tools to encourage their interest in writing. Long before a child ever writes distinct letters, she begins to copy the actions of someone who writes on paper. Once she has learned to identify letters and has the hand strength to hold a pencil correctly, true letter writing will follow.

Curiosity and Problem Solving

Curiosity is a natural instinct for children. Newborns turn their heads toward sounds and interesting faces. Once a child learns to crawl, she begins to move around her environment to touch the objects that she sees. Even into toddlerhood, she shakes and mouths toys to determine their texture and what they can do. Exploring the environment with her senses of vision, smell, taste, touch, and hearing allows her to take in more information, generate new questions, and then seek additional information to answer them. As children approach preschool age, they often begin seeking the causes and effects in their environments. What happens when the bucket in the sand table gets filled too far? What happens when I press harder with the crayon when I color? What happens when I mix the paint colors together?

How Teachers Can Help

Provide and Take Advantage of Learning Opportunities

Teachers and families can nurture children's curiosity. For teachers, one of the best ways to do this is to follow children's learning interests—the same practice that forms the basis of emergent curriculum. Just as adults do, children pay more attention to topics that interest them. If teachers take time to discover these topics and plan lessons on them, children will instinctively want to learn more.

Both teachers and family members can encourage children's curiosity by participating in the learning process themselves. Most young children model what they see the important adults in their lives doing, so a child is more apt to explore things that interest her when she sees adults pursuing additional knowledge. Adults can intentionally let children witness them reading, participating in back-and-forth conversations, and attempting to solve problems. Even better, an adult can tell a child about a simple problem in the classroom or home and explain how the adult is attempting to fix it.

 ## Case Study: Think-Aloud Troubleshooting

Five-year-old McKenna comes out of the bathroom and says, "Mommy, the toilet's broken." Her mother, Lisa, comes with her to investigate and discovers that the toilet does not flush when someone pushes the handle.

Seeing an opportunity to teach McKenna about problem solving, Lisa starts to narrate her own thoughts: "Well, this is a problem! How can I fix this? I know—I'll look on the internet. It has lots of articles about how to fix broken things." Lisa continues to describe her thought process to McKenna as she (Lisa) researches the issue online, unsuccessfully tries a few suggested fixes, and ends up calling a plumber.

Answer Questions

As any preschool teacher can tell you, three- and four-year-olds ask many questions every day. Though this behavior can prove annoying at times, it also presents an important opportunity to nurture curiosity. When adults answer her questions, a child continues to pursue information because her newly acquired knowledge leads to additional questions. But when adults constantly discourage a child from asking questions, she learns some perhaps-unintended social rules: "do not to talk to adults" or "asking questions is bad."

If a child asks a question that an adult cannot answer, it is perfectly acceptable to say, "I don't know." But instead of leaving it there, the adult should either look for the answer with the child or encourage further brainstorming by asking the child what she believes the answer may be. These actions help the child learn what to do if she does not get an answer from the first source she consults.

Have Open-Ended Conversations

Open-ended conversations make an excellent way to encourage curiosity and help a child learn to problem solve. These discussions rely heavily on open-ended questions and open-ended statements. *Open-ended questions* typically start with *how* or *why*—such as "How does that work?" or "Why do you think that happened?"—and need more than a one- or two-word answer. *Open-ended statements* often begin with lead-ins such as "Tell me about a time when . . ." or "I wonder what happens if . . ." Regardless of the exact words they use, the most important aspect of these questions and statements is that they do not have one correct answer, so a child can imagine many different possibilities.

Imagination and creativity are major parts of problem-solving, so teachers and family members need to nurture this skill in children. Open-ended conversations allow the child to communicate personal information, such as what she considers important or what is happening in her life, but they also allow her to imagine. Since an open-ended question does not require a one-word answer, children have the opportunity to explore a little more. For example, when an adult asks a child what her baby doll is thinking, the child is free to imagine what a baby would be concerned about and can attempt to describe that in her response. The adult can nurture this type of imagination by encouraging the child in responding, such as by asking what else baby dolls think about. By allowing the child to offer responses without worrying about whether they are right or wrong, teachers and families establish the foundation for further creativity.

Provide Open-Ended Materials

Another way to allow children to imagine and practice problem solving is to use open-ended materials. *Open-ended materials* do not require the child to use them in a specific way. A puzzle is not an open-ended material, because a child can only complete it by placing each piece in its designated spot. On the other hand, a child can arrange building blocks or Legos in any pattern she can think of, so both are open-ended materials.

Preschool teachers can provide children with as many open-ended materials as possible to encourage the learning process. Typically, these materials appear in the art, block, dramatic-play, and science centers and in social-studies materials. The following are some examples:

- Buttons
- Stones
- Shells
- Seeds
- Acorns
- Leaves
- Wooden craft sticks
- Toilet-paper tubes
- Torn pieces of paper
- Sequins

- Nuts and bolts
- Beads
- Yarn
- String
- Lids
- Clamps
- Clothespins
- Empty bottles
- Cardboard

Preacademic materials (literacy and math activities) often seek specific responses from a child, such as "What letter is this?" or "What does one plus one equal?" In contrast, science materials may give the child the opportunity to create experiments and brainstorm possible outcomes. Dramatic-play clothing and props allow children to act out many social situations and dream about what could happen to each character. These types of activities allow children to problem solve. For instance, a child in the science center might need to decide how to adjust an experiment to get the outcome she wants. In the dramatic-play center, if Mia dresses up as a shark and wants to "eat" Tariq, who's dressed up as an octopus, the children might need to figure out how to help the two characters get along.

Set Up the Classroom to Encourage Exploration

The way that a teacher sets up a classroom can prompt curiosity and exploration. When teachers frequently tell children that portions of the classroom are closed or that the children cannot use certain materials, children hesitate to explore. No one likes to be repeatedly shut down. Making the entire classroom available to children encourages them to explore until they find something interesting.

To make this setup work, teachers need to arrange materials so that children can access them independently. If children need adult help (which may take a long time to acquire in a classroom with up to ten children for every adult) to reach or set up the items they want, they cannot fully explore the room. By making it possible for children to investigate on their own, teachers demonstrate trust in the children, which builds their confidence. Confident children do seek out adults when they need help, but in general, they willingly try new tasks and learn about new things without assistance. When a child does not feel confident, she typically stays close to an adult and relies on her to initiate new experiences. Unfortunately, this limits the child's ability to learn, because the adult must divide her attention among all the children in the class and cannot exclusively focus on one child.

Have Realistic Expectations

Because every child learns at a different pace, many children will not come to kindergarten with preliteracy and prenumeracy skills mastered. The transition from preschool to kindergarten is particularly challenging for many children, so kindergarten teachers typically spend the first few months of the school year reviewing preacademic (literacy and numeracy) and other school-readiness skills. Once children are chronologically and developmentally mature enough, they typically learn letters and numbers quickly, but there will always be some students who struggle with these skills more than their peers do. Kindergarten teachers can provide additional support for students who need it; however, families and preschool teachers need to understand that implementing preliteracy and prenumeracy skills earlier and earlier in the early childhood curriculum is not the way to achieve school readiness. Children master skills when they are developmentally ready to do so, not after a certain number of exposures.

To use a somewhat silly analogy, imagine that Aria regularly sets her three-year-old son, Preston, in the front seat of her car to teach him how to drive. Aside from his being far too young to legally drive, Preston faces other critical obstacles to learning this skill, such as his inability to read street signs and his being too short to simultaneously reach the pedals and see over the dashboard. If Aria continues trying to teach Preston to drive at this time, both of them will end up frustrated. No matter how much Aria wants Preston to "get a head start" or "be ready for driving," she cannot make him learn this skill before he is physically and cognitively ready.

Similarly, no one benefits if preschool teachers try to force children to read, write, and count before they truly have the capacity to learn how. Preschool is not meant to teach children the skills that they will learn in kindergarten. Instead, preschool experiences need to focus on language, exploration, and social and emotional skills—the basic life skills that help children function so that they can learn academic skills. With the proper foundation, more children can enter kindergarten ready to succeed.

chapter 8

Emergent Curriculum and Developing Social and Emotional Skills

One of the key learning experiences a child has during preschool is mastering the social and emotional skills he needs for life in a classroom. Although children do not typically want to sit down and talk about emotions, children are naturally drawn to interact with peers and adults in the classroom. These interactions provide ideal opportunities to teach social and emotional skills. Teachers may model these types of skills, or they may directly teach them while mediating interactions between children.

Social and emotional skills will assist children throughout their education and well beyond. The process of learning these skills can take the majority of the preschool years. If someone provides in-home care for a child during this period, the child can easily build self-help and communication skills and progress in his cognitive development, but he may struggle to develop social skills because he does not spend much time in a group setting with other young children. Children must learn how to acclimate to a group environment and follow the rules of social order so that they can continue to succeed in school as they mature.

Overview of Preschoolers' Social and Emotional Development

Although social skills and emotional skills differ somewhat, they complement each other in the growth and development of the whole child. As mentioned in chapter 7, *social skills* enable a child to interact with others and to learn and follow the social rules of his environments. *Emotional skills* enable a child to identify, regulate, and express his emotions.

Typical Milestones

To understand best how a child must operate in the social environment of the classroom, all teachers need to understand typical social- and emotional-development milestones for preschoolers.

Three-Year-Old Child	Four-Year-Old Child	Five-Year-Old Child
• Can share toys and take turns with others • May show attachment to a close friend • Can initiate play with a friend or join a group when playing • Can follow the rules of a game but may be more interested in winning • Becomes less egocentric than a toddler • Becomes more cooperative with others but still throws tantrums when he cannot get his way • Begins participating in dramatic play; may act out a scene and pretend to be "Mommy" or "Daddy" • Can verbally express a broad range of emotions (for example, jealousy, anger, fear, joy, excitement) • Shows more independence than a toddler	• Begins to develop friendships • Starts to show awareness of other people's feelings • Can play games with simple rules • Can listen while others speak • Begins to understand the difference between right and wrong • Improves his ability to share and take turns • Can control frustration or anger during minor upsets • Can maintain attention for up to five minutes during adult-led activities, longer during play • Enjoys dramatic play with a group of peers • Becomes more concerned about what is fair and unfair	• Wants to please friends • Wants to be like friends • Can tell the difference between real and pretend • More likely than younger children to agree with rules and follow them • Can understand some gender-oriented traits • Can share willingly

Early education programs need to conduct regular screenings or assessments for all children. These evaluations show the most advanced skill that an individual child has mastered and what skills he is just beginning to learn. Then the teacher can assist the child with skills that are still challenging. By using this type of assessment, the teacher can pinpoint the needs of each child as an individual instead of estimating what the entire class needs. Furthermore, these screenings can play a key role in detecting developmental delays.

Delays in Social and Emotional Development

A teacher may be the first person to notice a child's struggle to develop social skills. With other developmental domains, such as motor skills and other aspects of physical development, the teacher and the child's family typically notice the same delays. However, difficulties with social skills may not present in the home in the same manner as they do in the classroom. Because a child may interact with few or no other young children at home, he may find the group environment of the classroom particularly challenging.

If a teacher mentions concerns about a child's social skills to the child's family members, a common response is, "I have never noticed that behavior before." This may sound like denial, but that is not necessarily the case. Because the home environment functions in a totally different manner than a preschool environment does—different people, different rules, different activities, even different values—the problematic behavior may simply not have arisen at home. In this situation, the teacher should help the family member reflect on settings where he has observed the child interacting with a group of other children, such as at a birthday party, the public library, or a place of worship. The family member may realize that he actually has seen the concerning behavior before—just not at home.

The following list provides some behaviors that might signal cause for concern about a child's social and emotional development:

- The child does not join in ongoing play with other children at an age when he typically would do so.
- The child does not initiate play with another child at an age when he typically would do so.
- The child depends on an adult to do everything with him instead of making independent choices.
- The child follows routines rigidly and cannot adapt to changes.
- The child shows extreme fear when separating from a trusted adult, beyond typical separation anxiety.
- The child acts completely unaware of others' feelings at an age when he typically would notice them. For example, four-year-old Yukio takes a doll away from his classmate Stella without asking. Stella starts to cry, but Yukio does not seem to notice.

- The child cannot develop friendships with others at an age when he typically would do so. For instance, four-year-old Balam only engages in dramatic play by himself. At this age, children typically play in groups for dramatic play, even if different children are acting out different story lines.

If a preschooler exhibits some of these social delays, his family might need to seek help from a pediatrician or speech-language pathologist. Because you do not have the specialized training needed to diagnose a child, approach these situations carefully. In *How Can I Help? A Teacher's Guide to Early Childhood Behavioral Health*, Ginger Welch recommends that you discuss the issue with an administrator first and then proceed cautiously to address the matter with the child's family. She further explains:

> If you suggest to family members in your official capacity that a child needs additional services (for example, if you say, "Your child has [diagnosis]. You need to take her to a doctor"), you could make your program liable to pay for those services. Use language that clearly shows that you are not requiring family members to take a particular action. For example, you might say, "I'm seeing [behavior that concerns you]. I suggest that you see [an applicable professional] to get more information."

You may want to keep a current list of local medical providers on hand in case the family asks you for a recommendation.

Tools for Promoting Social and Emotional Development

American sociologist Mildred Parten found that children move through six stages of play (which, as discussed in chapter 2, is how they learn) as they grow:

1. **Unoccupied play:** Children play and learn through unplanned exploration.
2. **Solitary play:** Children pick the toys and materials with which they wish to play. They play individually, but they may be physically close to others while playing.
3. **Onlooker play:** Children watch other children while they play, but the watchers do not interact with the players.
4. **Parallel play:** Children play with the same types of materials in the same area as other children, but they play individually. For instance, Jeff and Heidi both play with blocks in the block area, but Heidi builds a fort while Jeff builds a road.

5. **Associative play:** Children play with the same types of materials in the same area as others. They interact during play, but they do not play cooperatively. For instance, Rosie and Alana are sharing the kitchen toys in the dramatic-play area. While Rosie pretends to make a cake for her mother's birthday, Alana pretends to bake cookies with her grandmother.

6. **Cooperative play:** Children play together with the same types of materials, in the same area, and with the same end goal. For example, all the boys in the block area try to build the world's tallest tower together.

As children move through these stages of play, they begin to negotiate stronger relationships with others and problem solve to reach common goals. By the time children enter preschool, they are moving from the stage of only wanting to play by themselves to a point when they take interest in what others do in the classroom. In other words, they may be in either the stage of onlooker play or the stage of parallel play. Three-year-olds typically spend their first year in preschool learning how to begin functioning in a group environment. During their second preschool year, four-year-olds begin improving their social skills and even come to enjoy playing in groups.

As toddlers move into preschool and group play becomes common, teachers can rely on several important strategies to help children continue their social and emotional development.

Modeling

Young children need to see examples of what it looks like to play cooperatively in a group. The teacher should provide these models by sitting in the classroom play areas and participating in activities. For example, he can dress up and talk with children in the dramatic-play center. He can ask children to help him build a tower in the block area and have them offer suggestions on where the next block needs to go to make the tower taller. He can dance and shake streamers with the children in the music area.

Modeling also helps children learn the types of conversations that should take place between peers during play. For instance, if Quondra can zip up a costume independently, the teacher can show her how to offer to help other children with zippers, and he can show other children how to ask Quondra for assistance. The teacher can also show children how to work on a single project with multiple people. He might offer each child at the sensory table a magnifying glass and ask the children to find special items in the sand. As each child identifies something, the teacher can encourage all the children to listen to their peers and ask them additional questions.

Children do not learn these skills unless they see others using them. Team teachers need to model cooperative and conversation skills with one another. Many teachers believe that they should not speak to one another at all during the school day so that they can give their full attention to the children. Though teachers should not have personal conversations while

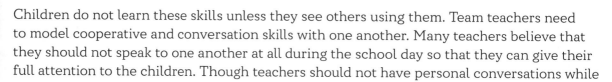

children are in the room, teachers also need to model skills for the children throughout the school day. During family-style dining, for instance, the teachers need to demonstrate how to serve themselves and pass food politely around the table. Both with each other and with the children, they also need to model how to have typical mealtime conversation, as many children may not participate in family meals at home.

Working at Each Child's Pace

Most skills, including social and emotional ones, can be charted on a continuum from complete ignorance of a certain skill to mastery of it. Just as with every other skill set, children develop along the continua of social and emotional skills at their own paces. Still, the wait for this growth can be difficult, because challenging behaviors usually develop during the process. For example, preschoolers may still have tantrums as they learn self-regulation. Fights may erupt in the classroom among children who are still learning how to share or interact with others. Children who have not yet learned to follow simple directions may cause injury to themselves or others in the classroom or on the playground. These types of problems can cause considerable stress for classroom staff, especially because family members often do not see the same behaviors at home and may react with skepticism when told about them. At the same time, unless preschool teachers intervene, these behaviors will make it much harder for children to do well in kindergarten.

To help a child with challenging behavior prepare to succeed in school, the teacher must first identify what social or emotional skill the child is struggling with (there may be more than one) and where the child is on the developmental continuum for that skill. Then the teacher must determine how to help the child advance along the continuum. For example, if a child has difficulty playing with others, the teacher may need to help him learn how to identify and express his own emotions so he can interact well in a group. If a child struggles to separate from a family member each morning, the teacher might work on establishing a strong relationship with the child so that he feels safe at school without the family member present. In this case, once the child feels safe, he may quickly move along the continua for other social and emotional skills.

Arranging the Classroom

Teachers can encourage social and emotional development through the ways in which they arrange their classrooms. The classroom should have areas that encourage group play and areas that allow students to be alone. More-social centers, such as the dramatic-play and block areas, need to include enough space so that several students can play together without being crowded, thus helping prevent pushing and arguments. The classroom also needs at least one area where any child can go to be alone when he feels overstimulated or overwhelmed. Having a safe space to calm down away from the rest of the group can help prevent many episodes of hitting, throwing toys, having tantrums, or other challenging behaviors.

Key Social and Emotional Skills to Teach in the Classroom

Arguably, preschoolers learn far more social and emotional skills than academic ones in their classrooms. While this concerns some family members who worry about school readiness, these skills lay important foundations for children's lives. For instance, many of the soft skills that employers look for in potential hires are behaviors and practices that children typically learn before age five. Children must learn how to work cooperatively in a group. They need to learn how to read others' emotions and respond appropriately. Children need to learn to share space and materials with others in a common area and how to follow an agreed-upon set of rules. All these skills are essential throughout school and in the workforce. Similarly, a child will need these skills throughout his life to build successful relationships with friends, teachers, coworkers, romantic partners, and others. Because everyone needs to learn social and emotional skills, teachers must spend a significant portion of classroom time teaching them, even though these activities do not result in tangible end products.

Holding Conversations

In a world in which people interact largely on screens, early childhood educators have to teach children essential conversation skills. For instance, children do not naturally know how to greet people—adults must teach them. Teachers can model greetings as families come into the classroom each morning and as the class sits down together at circle time. Teach children to initiate a greeting with spoken words such as "Hello" or "How are you?" Show them how to use tone and body language to show that they are excited to see someone and to begin speaking. Because many children now stare frequently at a screen, emphasize the importance of making eye contact in greetings and conversations, as appropriate in each child's culture. Explain that in mainstream American culture, looking someone in the eye shows respect because it demonstrates that you are giving the person your full attention.

Once individuals have greeted each other, then what happens? Teachers need to show children how to start and maintain a back-and-forth conversation. Once a child asks a question, the teacher needs to help him understand how that question can develop into a conversation. This entails more than just talking; it also involves giving attention to what a peer says and not interrupting. Family-style dining offers a wonderful opportunity to demonstrate back-and-forth conversation, though any time of the school day can work. Free play, for instance, is a great time to join in the children's activities so you can practice back-and-forth conversations with individuals and small groups. Regardless of the timing, the key is to teach children to show interest while another person talks and to respond to what he says instead of only telling their own stories. Demonstrate full eye contact and engaged body language—turning your body to face the speaker, nodding occasionally, and so on—when each person speaks, and encourage others to give their attention to the speaker.

Some children may have advanced conversation skills because they have lots of conversations in their homes, but other students may need additional modeling. Along with your own demonstrations, try pairing peer role models with students who need more practice with conversation skills. Watching and learning from a peer can provide a powerful lesson.

Listening

Children learn several different types of listening skills in their preschool years, so teachers spend a great deal of time working on this developmental goal. Of course, children need to learn how to listen to verbal directions so they can complete tasks independently. All preschools, including ones that use emergent curriculum, start by teaching children to follow one-step and eventually two-step directions. As children learn to follow directions, teachers should avoid battles for control. It can help for teachers to include many requests within daily routines and transitions, such as cleaning up toys when certain music plays in the classroom. This type of strategy can teach children to listen to directions without starting a power struggle.

Conversations require a different type of listening. This skill relates to empathy: as children become less egocentric, they begin to see that just as they want others to listen to them when they speak, other children and adults have the same desire. Listening in a conversation requires participants to process not just the speaker's words but also his tone and facial expressions in order to grasp the full meaning of the communication. This is a lot for a young child to do all at the same time, so he will need adult help to learn how. During teacher-student interactions, teachers need to model listening to a conversation partner's complete statement before speaking. If the child interrupts, the teacher can prompt him to finish listening or can ask him if he heard what the speaker said before the interruption.

Furthermore, teachers need to explain that some conversations have unique expectations for listening. When an adult, particularly a family member or a teacher, asks a child to listen, it has different implications than if a peer makes the same request. According to the norms of mainstream American culture, the child needs to respect an adult as an authority figure and do as he asks. In contrast, the child does not have the same level of obligation to comply when a peer asks him to listen, but it is polite to do so.

Because a child typically begins to read others' emotions during the preschool years, he may already have the necessary skills to be a good listener. He may just need to watch an adult model the behavior of listening, or he might need an adult to explain the process. For instance, preschoolers may already know that they need to be quiet while someone else speaks, but they might not know that they need to listen to that person to determine what to do or say next. Try teaching and modeling these skills in the dramatic-play area while acting out a story. You could also have a small group role-play a social narrative and then ask the children how to handle that situation.

Case Study: Turning a Quarrel into a Lesson

While playing in the house in the dramatic-play center, Marie and Luz begin fighting over the dress-up clothes. Their teacher, Odessa, recognizes this situation as an opportunity to teach them about social skills. She takes both girls aside and prompts them to have a conversation by saying, "I can tell that Marie really wants to tell us something. Let's listen and see what she needs to say."

Once Marie has had the opportunity to talk, Odessa turns to her and says, "I can tell that Luz was listening to you. I wonder what she thought about what you had to say." Then Odessa asks Luz to share her thoughts.

Showing Empathy and Apologizing

Empathy is a challenging skill to teach. Young children are naturally egocentric and worry about their own needs first, but empathy requires them to look at a situation from another person's perspective. Fortunately for teachers, preschoolers are just beginning to identify the emotions associated with other people's facial expressions, and this new ability can provide a starting point for conversations about empathy.

For instance, as any early childhood teacher can testify, young children squabble frequently. While mediating such a disagreement, you can initiate a lesson on empathy by posing a calm question to a student, such as "Can you look at your friend's face and tell me what you think he is feeling?" or "What feelings do you have right now? Do you think your friend has the same kinds of feelings?" If the child has trouble with this exercise, try consulting one of the many excellent children's books that include pictures of facial expressions and descriptions of the emotions associated with those expressions. These books also make superb tools for large-group reading or for individual children who need additional support to identify feelings.

During this type of exercise, sometimes a child concludes that his actions have upset a peer or an adult. In these cases, the social rules of mainstream American culture dictate that the child should apologize. Offer him this option, but do not force him to apologize. A sincere apology must have empathy attached to it—the child should realize that his actions have harmed someone else, and he should feel remorse for that behavior. An apology is a way to show that remorse. If the child does not feel sorry for his actions, he is not truly ready to offer an apology, and forcing him to do so anyway will provide a model of insincerity. Although the teacher may desperately want the children to resolve their disagreement, he must give them the option to sort through their own emotions first, especially because an apology will likely stir up new emotions.

Younger preschoolers may not be developmentally ready to understand empathy, so adults should not expect them to do so, but children of this age can still learn from seeing the teacher model empathy and explain his thinking. You might say, "I'm looking at Enzo's face, and I can tell he's sad because he's frowning. I know that when I'm sad, I feel better when someone hugs me. Enzo, would you like a hug?" Just hearing the teacher talk through this process may help build the foundation that a young preschooler needs to eventually understand empathy.

Developing Self-Confidence

As preschoolers begin to show more independence, they begin to develop self-confidence. *Self-confidence* is a feeling that arises when children recognize their own competence at certain activities. Of course, no child or even adult is competent at everything, and that is okay! But some adults praise everything a child does as if he did have such superhuman abilities. Teachers and families need to be honest and transparent with young children to help them develop a healthy sense of competence.

As each child begins to feel independent, his teachers and family members should allow him to make decisions whenever possible. The adults will remain the decision-makers when it comes to matters of health and safety, such as whether a child may climb on top of the monkey bars instead of swinging across them. But if a child can choose what he wants for dinner or what to play next, he begins to feel more empowered in his environment.

As part of making these decisions, a preschooler can and should take healthy risks. For instance, try letting a five-year-old pour his own milk, build a block tower as high as he can, or taste a new food. If he spills his milk, he can clean it up. If he knocks his tower down, he can build it better next time. If he finds salsa too spicy, he can choose to not eat it again. Taking these risks will not hurt him, and they help him set boundaries in his mind for what he can and cannot do. On the other hand, if he pours his milk without spilling it, he can take pride in that simple victory. In his mind, that is something worth celebrating because he did it independently even though he could have made a mistake.

Teachers and family members can help children develop self-confidence in other ways. First, avoid giving a child generic praise for every action regardless of success or failure. Overusing terms such as *great* and *awesome* makes true praise lose its value. If a child succeeds at a task, compliment him on specific things he did well, such as by saying, "I can tell that you worked hard to make your bed, and you put everything in the right place." If a child fails, acknowledge that without being punitive. You might say something such as, "It's okay that you made a mistake and spilled the milk. All you need to do is clean it up." Be honest about what happened so that the child understands what true success in that task looks like.

As children begin to take more risks and attempt independence, teachers and families need to create school and home environments that make children feel safe. To take risks, a child needs to know that adults will still love and accept him if he fails. Thus, regardless of what happens when a child takes a risk, show affection to him. If the risk could have hurt him or others, such as riding a tricycle so fast that he lost control and almost crashed, explain why the child should not repeat that choice, but reiterate that you love him anyway. No child will ever develop true self-confidence unless he feels unconditional love and acceptance from the most important adults in his life.

Solving Problems

Problem solving often plays a large part in social interactions. When two children enter an exchange with different wants and needs and subsequently end up in an argument, they need to devise a solution to the problem. With younger preschoolers, an adult typically mediates the conversation, offers two acceptable ways to resolve the situation, and allows the children to pick one. With older preschoolers, who have more highly developed language skills and can often brainstorm together, the adult may simply stand close by in the event that the children need him during the discussion. The children's temperaments may also help determine how much he assists.

As with listening and apologizing, empathy is key to helping children decide how to solve a social problem. For instance, if a teacher can help Ruru identify how his actions have hurt LaVon, Ruru may sincerely want to help find a solution because of remorse. On the other hand, if Ruru does not show any remorse, he may only be worried about whether the situation is "fair" (as he sees it). In such cases, teachers can assist a great deal by talking through social narratives with the children. LaVon and Ruru's teacher could say, "Ruru, if someone took your toy away, how would you feel? What would make you feel better?" Even if a child is not developmentally ready to show empathy on his own, an adult can still explain how to see another person's perspective.

Following Social Rules

Every environment has social rules that dictate behavior so that the environment remains safe and orderly. Sometimes an authority figure posts or explicitly states the rules; sometimes they are only implied, so people have to discover them on their own. For instance, swimming pools usually post signs that instruct everyone to walk, not run, to prevent slips, falls, and possible injuries or drownings. On the other hand, houses of worship do not typically post lists of rules, but by observing leaders and other attendees, a visitor can discern that he should dress somewhat formally and talk softly to show respect.

Similarly, early childhood classrooms have social rules that explain what is and is not appropriate behavior there. Teachers must help children learn how to discover and follow those rules, as children will need to use these skills throughout their lives.

Most early childhood classrooms formally establish certain rules from the beginning of the school year. These rules typically include several of the following:

- Use gentle hands (do not hit).
- Use walking feet (do not run).
- Use soft voices when inside (do not scream).
- Feet go on the floor (do not climb on furniture).
- Use your ears for listening.
- Take turns.

Of course, all these rules seem reasonable to adults, but it takes time for young children to develop the self-regulation to comply, especially if they have not encountered such structured rules before entering preschool. To help children master classroom social rules, teachers can use these strategies:

- **Phrase the rules in a way that explains what children *should* do instead of what they *should not* do.** When a teacher tells a child, "Don't climb on that bookshelf," the child can instantly stop climbing on that bookshelf, but he does not necessarily know what to do instead. Can he climb on the table, or is all climbing off limits? Positively worded rules tell children specifically what their teachers expect from them. This phrasing also prevents teachers from having to constantly use negative words, such as *stop*, *don't*, and *no*, to remind children of the rules.
- **Ask the children to help develop the rules.** When children help create rules, they tend to comply better because they have a stake in the matter. Typically, children have some knowledge of what they should and should not do in the classroom, so they offer many good ideas for the rules. If a child offers a potentially overly restrictive idea, the teacher can talk through the proposal with the class to see whether that idea would make an appropriate rule. For example, a child suggests this rule: "No one can hang their backpack in Kaitlyn's cubby." That idea is a little too specific to be part of the overall classroom rules, but the teacher could guide the children from it to the idea of returning items to their proper places. If the children offer only negative rules, such as "Don't run" or "Don't hit," then the teacher can ask for suggestions of what the children should do instead of running or hitting.

Beyond learning the classroom rules, preschool children are also learning the social structure of the room. This means learning about general social rules that people use in group settings. They must learn who is in charge in the classroom and whether specific individuals have social statuses. For instance, if an adult comes to volunteer in the classroom, the children should listen to him, but he is not the teacher. Sometimes teachers unintentionally convey that certain social rules are firm and others are suggestions, leading children to think things such as, "Do I really have to stay on my mat at nap time, or can I wander around the room without getting in trouble?" Children also can discover which teachers are more sympathetic to them, whom they would rather seek comfort from, and whom they want to tattle to when others break the rules. Although these behaviors often frustrate teachers, they do show that children are learning to use observation and reasoning skills to determine how the classroom environment works. It also means that the teachers may need to more consistently maintain the same rules for every child every day.

chapter 9

Emergent Curriculum and Developing Handwriting Skills

Families often identify writing one's own name as the most essential kindergarten-readiness skill. They may even question preschool teachers about when children will achieve this milestone. These families may not understand that to write her name on paper, a child has to combine many abilities: fine motor skills, visual skills, sensory processing, attention, executive function, organization, posture, and eye-hand coordination. Each of these skills takes a long time to develop, often beginning as early as toddlerhood. An effective preschool teacher needs to provide a classroom environment where a young child has plenty of opportunities to build each ability before being expected to write her name.

Setting Realistic Goals for Young Writers

Handwriting refers to the act of writing words on paper by hand. To develop classroom environments where children can learn this skill, preschool teachers need to understand the developmental stages through which children move when learning to write letters. The following table explains what prehandwriting skills a child develops during each stage.

Birth to Six Months	• Child watches her hands move and brings them to her mouth • Child swings whole arm at object of interest • Child tracks a person with her eyes as the person moves across a room • Child begins to hold small objects, such as a rattle, with a fist • Child begins to bring both hands together • Child begins passing objects from one hand to the other
Six to Twelve Months	• Child begins holding onto objects • Child begins to use index finger to poke at objects • Child begins to explore texture of objects • Child plays with her own hands • Child begins to eat finger food • Child can place small objects in a cup • Child can hold two small objects in one hand • Child can hold a crayon with a fist

Twelve to Eighteen Months	• Child begins to show some preference for right or left hand, but hand dominance is not decided • Child can clap hands together • Child can wave goodbye • Child can stack two blocks in a tower • Child can scribble with a crayon on paper
Eighteen Months to Two Years	• Child begins to hold objects, such as a crayon, with the fingertips and thumb • Child can remove pegs from a pegboard • Child can build a tower with three to four blocks • Child can turn pages in a book
Two Years	• Child can move and shape playdough • Child can string large beads on a string • Child can turn a doorknob to open a door • Child can use a spoon correctly • Child can wash her own hands
Three Years	• Child can use scissors to cut paper • Child can unbutton large buttons • Child can manipulate a shoelace through lacing cards • Child can sort small objects • Child can draw a circle after watching an adult model it
Four Years	• Child shows a dominant hand • Child can complete simple puzzles • Child can touch the tip of each finger to her thumb • Child can use a fork correctly • Child can get dressed and undressed independently

Five Years	• Child can cut out circles • Child can hold a pencil or crayon correctly • Child can write her own name • Child can draw a person with five to six body parts • Child can draw a square and a triangle
Six Years	• Child can stay on a line when cutting with scissors • Child can independently complete a puzzle of fifteen to twenty pieces • Child can build small structures with blocks • Child can write all letters of the alphabet and numerals 0 through 9

When preschool teachers and family members want a three-year-old to write her name, they expect her to have in place many different skill sets that are not developmentally appropriate for her age. Not only does she not recognize all letters yet, but she also does not yet have the muscle development, the hand-eye coordination, or the visual perception skills to complete this type of task. Some children may reach these developmental milestones earlier than others, but it is not appropriate to expect that result for an entire classroom of preschoolers.

Preparing Children to Learn to Write

A child's environment, experiences, and interest in writing all affect when she will be ready to learn to write. Although some children may be ready at age four or five, other children may not have the needed motor skills or preliteracy skills until closer to age six. For children who are not yet ready for writing, teachers can use prehandwriting activities in the classroom. Sometimes, however, a teacher finds that some children do not have even the basic fine motor skills necessary for these activities, so she may need to implement some additional activities to help the children build those skills. The following sections describe activities that can help all children prepare for writing.

Developing Hand Strength

Motor skills are the foundation of learning handwriting. To understand how motor skills affect a child's ability to write, let's examine how a typically developing body builds its large and small muscle groups. Researcher Laura Berk explains that child development is *cephalocaudal* (from top to bottom) and *proximodistal* (from the core to the extremities). We can see this easily with infants. A child begins to lift her head at about two months old, but she does not learn to walk until around her first birthday. At four months old, an infant has the core muscles to begin rolling over, but the muscles in her fingers are not mostly developed until she is five or six years old.

When children begin to learn handwriting, they start with building posture skills to help them sit up straight and control the core muscles of the body. According to researcher Steve Sanders, these muscles create balance, and balance allows children to move safely and control their bodies. Children need balance skills to sit still, hold a piece of paper still, and make controlled movements with a pencil. Some children struggle more with balance than with moving freely, because movement may require less control than balance.

To help children improve their balance skills, preschool teachers should include activities for building gross motor skills in the daily classroom routine. Besides developing their core muscles, children need to build strength in their arms and legs so they can achieve the best posture for sitting at a table and writing. Several gross motor activities that can help improve handwriting include the following:

- Wheelbarrow walking
- Animal walks (for example, bear walks or crab walks)
- Beanbag games
- Chair or wall push-ups
- Yoga
- Tug-of-war
- Air writing letters using the whole arm
- Climbing activities on the playground or on hanging ropes
- Swinging from monkey bars
- Large art projects that are hung on the wall so that a child has to use her entire arm to paint strokes or use a marker

Once a child has strong core muscles and balance skills, the teacher needs to find ways to help create stronger muscles in the fingers. This may begin with improving the child's grasp to make not only the fingers but also the entire hand stronger. Playdough and modeling clay, which is firmer, make excellent tools to improve grasp and finger strength. Children can use their hands to manipulate the dough, or they can use tools such as rolling pins and cookie cutters. Other similar options include playing with Silly Putty, slime, or Goobleck. Children can also strengthen their hand muscles by using tools such as chopsticks, tongs, and tweezers to transfer items from one container to another or to sort objects. The playground monkey bars can also strengthen palm strength just as much as they affect core muscle development.

To develop full finger strength, children must practice activities that help them develop a pincer grasp and a tripod grasp. These grasps involve intricate muscle movements, so they take repetition to master. Sample fine motor activities for the preschool classroom include the following:

- Tearing paper
- Playing games with clothespins
- Screwing and unscrewing jar lids
- Playing with pegboards
- Sorting small objects
- Stringing beads
- Using lacing cards
- Doing basic sewing
- Doing puzzles
- Playing with Knobbed Cylinders (a Montessori item)
- Using tweezers to transfer objects
- Making art with eyedroppers
- Painting or drawing on an easel
- Hammering golf tees into clay
- Playing with pipe cleaners
- Using interlocking blocks, such as Duplos and Legos
- Opening locks with keys
- Playing in sensory bins and sand trays
- Doing fingerplays and clapping games
- Playing board games that use fine motor skills, such as Kerplunk and Jenga
- Working with Sandpaper Letters (a Montessori item)
- Using dressing boards with Velcro, snaps, zippers, and buttons

Teaching Letter Recognition

Before a child has the hand strength to write with paper and pencil, she can begin to identify what letters look like and how they are created. Children must see letters and words throughout the classroom environment to become familiar with them. The teacher can label each material in the classroom with a printed word and a picture to help children learn key sight words. She can also post classroom rules and other key pieces of information throughout the classroom at the children's eye level. Each classroom should have enough books for each child to have access to printed reading materials, which means having at least one book for each child and potentially more, depending on how quickly the children look at every book available.

Once children have repeatedly seen letters and have begun to identify them, the teacher can begin to find unique methods for children to recreate those letters, even though the children do not yet have the hand muscles to make intricate movements with a tripod grasp on a pencil. For example, a teacher can place a model of a letter *A* on the same table as playdough. Children can roll the playdough into a long cylinder and then place it in the shape of an *A*. Using the playdough helps improve hand strength but is less challenging than using a pencil. Alternatively, the teacher can provide magnetic boards and long strips and curves of magnetic tape to place on the boards in the shapes of letters.

Montessori schools frequently use a shallow tray of sand in which a child can use her index finger to trace a letter. The texture of the sand offers an additional sensory experience along with the literacy activity. Montessori programs also use materials called Sandpaper Letters that have a similar purpose. As explained on the website Montessorium, Sandpaper Letters are made by cutting alphabet letters out of high-grit sandpaper and mounting them on small, flat pieces of wood. A child traces the sandpaper with her fingers to learn the formation of each letter.

Handwriting without Tears, a popular handwriting curriculum, uses wooden pieces in the shapes of lines and curves, which can be placed on a template to help students learn how to shape letters. Once children have mastered using the templates, they can use the wooden pieces to create the letters without the templates. This curriculum also uses small chalkboards to help children learn to shape the letters. A child uses a small, wet, cube-shaped sponge to trace the letters on a chalkboard, an activity that also helps her learn to use a successful pincer grasp to hold onto the sponge.

All these strategies help children learn to create letters even before they have the hand strength for traditional paper-and-pencil activities. When children experiment with the formation of letters, they can learn the differences between letters that look similar, such as *b* and *d*. All the time spent with exploration also allows children to improve their visual processing for more formal writing in the future.

Beyond teaching letter formation—which is essential so that children get into the habit of forming letters correctly—teachers also need to create materials that help students understand where letters should start on a piece of paper, how much space to leave between them, and how to organize them. For instance, Handwriting without Tears places a yellow sticker in the top left-hand corner of each page in its material to reinforce that letters always start at the top and move down. Montessori schools begin teaching the concepts of left to right and top to bottom with every material in the classroom. Even if a child scrubs a table with soap and water, she starts in the top left-hand corner, moves across the top, and then starts over on an imaginary row slightly below the starting point. These small cues in materials and practices prepare children to read and write from a young age.

Building on Emergent Writing

Long before they begin to write words, children learn to draw pictures to tell stories. This is an important step in the process of learning to write. First, for both writing and drawing, the child must develop the fine motor skills to manipulate the writing tool. Second, the child must think about what she wants to communicate with her pictures so she knows what to draw, just as she will eventually need to think about what she wants to say so she knows what letters to write.

Once the child takes more interest in actual handwriting, she begins by creating scribbles that look more like symbols than like a drawing. She might, for example, make lines of scribbles that start at the top of the page and move down to the bottom of the page. Over time, the scribbles gradually morph into letter-like forms. The "letters" may have parallel and horizontal lines, but they do not resemble the true alphabet letters used in English.

As soon as a child begins to produce true alphabet letters, she begins to write strings of letters in random patterns that resemble sentences but have no true meaning. By this time in her life, she has seen enough print to model what words and sentences look like, but she has not learned how to decode the letters so she can place them in a form that makes sense. However, at this same time, she learns the sounds associated with each letter of the alphabet. As soon as she masters these sounds, she can begin to group sounds together to create invented spellings of words. Because English has many exceptions to its spelling rules and only a small percentage of its words are spelled phonetically (that is, spelled the way they sound), children frequently spell their early written words incorrectly. However, a child's invented spelling will closely model a phonetic version of a word.

During preschool, children are often exposed to *sight words,* simple words the children should be able to identify by sight before they can sound out words. Because a child learns them by memory instead of sounding them out, they will be some of the first true words that she writes. She can even combine two or three sight words to form simple sentences, such as "I do."

Once children have begun to use invented spelling and recognize sight words, they are well on their way to writing stories and using conventional spelling and sentences. During this stage, children may constantly ask teachers how to spell certain words. Understandably, this can quickly become tedious for teachers. Remember that just as adults need to encourage a child's curiosity by answering her questions, they also need to encourage her interest in writing by telling her how to spell words when she asks.

Journaling

Even before children can spell words and create sentences, they can begin journaling. A journal for a preschooler may start off as pictures that the child draws, accompanied by captions that she dictates to a teacher. As the child learns more about writing, she may begin to write random selections of letters with her pictures, or she may attempt to copy words that she sees in the classroom environment. Even if the child does not yet write in a traditional style, she is learning to write in a journal in the same manner that she would read a book (from the top to the bottom of the page and from the front to the back of the book). You can use journals as a small-group activity that children do at regular times throughout the week, or you can make journals available to students to use whenever they would like to document their artwork or writing.

Besides helping children practice their writing and drawing skills, journals have several other benefits. First, they allow children to begin written communication through pictures. Children can find a way to express a point with colors, individual letters, captions dictated to teachers, or their first written words. Additionally, journals allow children to express a variety of emotions that they may not have the vocabulary to express. Thus, journals can assist with self-regulation and calming down; for example, you can have students draw the way that they feel. Even if students do not use the same journal throughout the year, keep scrap paper or small booklets available throughout the room for children to use for writing in every center. This practice can give students some of the same benefits as journaling. It also creates a language-rich environment for the children in which they can start to see how reading and writing can help them learn about all other content areas.

Transitioning to Paper and Pencil

As they grow, young children eventually will develop the skills to sit in chairs at tables and write with pencil and paper. When this time comes, teachers can rearrange the classroom if needed to better support writing practice. For instance, tables and chairs need to be the appropriate size for children. A child's feet should rest firmly on the floor (not barely reach it or dangle), and she should have a ninety-degree angle between her back and her lap and a ninety-degree angle between her lap and her shins. This support enables the child to maintain proper posture, which gives her better balance and increased ability to control the core muscles of the body.

The child's writing tool is also important. Because children have small hands, they often have trouble holding a large pencil or marker. The longer the writing tool is, the more weight it puts on a child's hand. Children can more easily manipulate a shorter-than-average tool, such as a golf pencil.

Preschool teachers also need to think about a child's physical endurance for writing. A track coach would not expect a sprinter to have the endurance to run a marathon. Similarly, if a child has never had to regularly sit down and write for an extended period of time, her hand muscles do not have the conditioning to sustain that level of work. They soon start to cramp and feel sore and eventually begin to spasm. At this point, the child is no longer creating her best work, which will likely frustrate both her and the teacher. If this pattern continues, the soreness may even cause the child to dislike or dread writing.

When a teacher encourages a child to write, the child should need to offer only a small sample of writing, such as writing a single letter or her first name. This will result in higher-quality work and will not harm the child's attitude toward handwriting. It also ensures that the child still has the freedom to move around the room and play. Even for an older preschooler, handwriting should take up only a tiny portion of the school day, and she should still have ample time to explore the room and engage in hands-on learning.

What If a Child Won't Write?

Many teachers wonder what to do if a child refuses to do handwriting activities. This often happens for one of three reasons. First, the child may not yet have the hand strength to complete the activity in question, so attempting it causes her discomfort, tension, or pain in her hands. To make matters worse, forcing a young child to repeat such negative learning experiences can taint her attitude about school for many years to come. Young children typically love coming to school to learn and play with friends, and we do not want to dampen that enthusiasm. So even if a child does not yet have the hand strength to write, teachers should still supply materials in the classroom that help her with letter recognition and fine motor development. The child can interact with those materials until her hand muscles are prepared for writing.

Second, a child may not want to complete a handwriting assignment because she does not want to sit down for tabletop activities. Many preschoolers need a lot of movement to help them learn, and they do not yet have the attention span to focus on a stationary activity such as handwriting for long periods. As with any activity in emergent curriculum, the teacher needs to incorporate the students' interests into handwriting tasks to encourage the children to participate. For instance, if a child shows interest in learning about sharks, the teacher might suggest a group project to create a book about sharks.

Third, a child may refuse to participate in handwriting activities because she is not developmentally ready to complete this type of work. For instance, she may not yet have the ability to sit still at a table long enough to complete the task. As with children with insufficiently developed hand strength, the teacher should help the child focus on letter-recognition activities and fine motor development. Then, once she is ready for tabletop work, she will already have begun working on important writing-related skills.

Remember that each child develops at a difference pace. Some children may not be prepared to begin handwriting work until they reach age five or six. Teachers should attempt to motivate children to try new and even difficult things, but pushing a child to do something beyond her developmental level will usually frustrate her, which hinders the learning process instead of advancing it.

chapter 10

Emergent Curriculum and Developing Problem-Solving Skills

To succeed in kindergarten, young children need to become independent thinkers. Skills such as memorizing letters, numbers, and colors or writing one's name are helpful for elementary school, but they do not have the same long-term impact as teaching children to analyze and solve problems as the children develop. When a child can identify a problem, determine its source, and suggest a way to solve the problem, he does not need the immediate assistance of an adult to handle the issue. He can create his own theories and test them in real time. Though the challenges a young child faces may seem simple, such as two peers fighting over the same set of blocks, learning how to solve these problems will assist him throughout his education and the rest of his life.

Piaget's Theory

To help children learn how to solve problems instead of just memorize information, early childhood educators need to understand how young children learn. Renowned Swiss psychologist Jean Piaget believed that each child passes through four stages of cognitive development on the way to developing executive functioning in the brain. Certain problem-solving skills develop in each stage, and a child must master the skills of one stage before moving on to the next.

In the following list, the information on each stage is taken from Piaget, the article "Newborn Reflexes" by the American Academy of Pediatrics, and the Child Development Institute.

Sensorimotor Stage

The *sensorimotor stage* lasts approximately from birth to age two.

- A baby initially responds to his environment with innate reflexes, such as rooting (turning his head when something brushes his cheek).
- Between two and four months old, the baby learns to intentionally repeat actions that he enjoys, such as kicking his legs when happy.
- Between four and eight months old, the baby begins to repeat actions that trigger enjoyable reactions within the environment. For example, he will shake a rattle over and over because he likes hearing the sound.
- Toward the end of his first year, the baby becomes more intentional in his actions. To continue the previous example, he will now pursue his rattle if it is out of reach, crawling toward it and pushing another object out of the way to reach it.
- Between twelve and eighteen months old, the now-toddler begins to learn by piecing objects together, whereas he previously only took them apart. He may try to stack blocks or place rings on top of a ring tower. These activities help him continue to develop intentionality in learning about his environment.

- Between eighteen months and two years old, the toddler learns how to visualize objects that are not physically present. Once the child has mastered this skill, he can develop *object permanence*: the understanding that an object still exists even when he cannot see it.

Preoperational Stage

The *preoperational stage* lasts approximately from age two to age seven. Most preschoolers are in this stage, although children with developmental delays may still be in the sensorimotor stage.

- The child exhibits *centration*, or focusing on only one element of a situation at a time. When an event is complex and has many different components, he will most likely focus on only one component. For instance, Olivia falls out of her chair, accidentally bumps Zane on the way down, and hits her head on the floor. Though Zane did not get hurt, he is upset that Olivia bumped him and keeps complaining about it. He does not seem to notice Olivia crying on the floor.
- The child is *egocentric*: he typically believes that his viewpoint is the most important and that others view situations in the same manner that he does. For example, Carli needs one more L-shaped block for her block tower. A few feet away, Jalen and Nox are also building a block tower, and they have used three L-shaped blocks. Because Carli needs another L-shaped block, she pulls one out of Jalen and Nox's tower without considering how the boys might feel about her action or what might happen to their tower.
- The child begins to use symbols to represent other things. He learns to identify letters and numbers, because he now can understand that, for example, the numeral *9* represents a given number of objects. At the beginning of the preoperational stage, the child can only memorize the names of letters, but toward the middle of this stage, he begins to associate a letter with a sound and can start to decode words.
- At the beginning of the preoperational stage, the child plays in the same room as other children but does not interact with them during play. As he masters more language skills and becomes less egocentric, he begins to engage in group play. Eventually the child begins to participate in *dramatic play*, in which he pretends to be a character other than himself.
- The child often demonstrates *animism*, or the belief that inanimate objects, particularly objects in nature, have thoughts and feelings similar to those of humans.

Concrete Operational Stage

The *concrete operational stage* lasts approximately from age seven to age eleven. Although most children do not reach this stage in preschool, a child can move ahead of his peers and advance to this level earlier than is typical.

- The child's thought process becomes highly logical. He can perform more-advanced operations in his head, including mathematical operations and other problem-solving processes, without the use of manipulatives to help work out the problems.
- The child learns *conservation*, or the concept that the same quantity still exists even if it is grouped differently. For instance, if an adult shows him a pile of ten coins and then spreads them out into a single line, the child understands that there are still the same number of coins, whereas a child in the preoperational stage might believe that there are more coins in the line than in the pile.

Formal Operational Stage

The *formal operational stage* lasts from approximately age eleven through the end of life. In this stage, the child learns to think and problem solve abstractly. Interestingly, Piaget theorized that many people do not achieve this stage and that they may need concrete information throughout adulthood to solve problems and make decisions.

Developing Curiosity and a Love of Learning

Because children take in a great deal of information between birth and age seven, it is the perfect time to establish a love of learning. This process begins with infants and toddlers, who are naturally curious about the world around them. The most important thing that family members and caregivers can do for children during these early years is encourage their curiosity. Let toddlers explore the environment. Encourage small children to ask questions. Curiosity is an essential skill for young children, and preschool teachers need to be prepared to encourage curiosity so that children develop a love of learning. Here are some ideas to try.

Set Up Exploration-Friendly Classrooms

Set up a classroom environment that allows children to explore. They should be allowed to touch and interact with all materials. Avoid frequently closing off areas of the classroom or prohibiting the use of certain materials at certain times of day. Of course, you may need to limit how many children play in a certain area at a time to avoid overcrowding and arguments. But if you say no to a certain kind of play merely because you do not want to clean up that area of the classroom afterward, perhaps you should rethink that decision.

A classroom should have enough blocks and other toys to make sure that all children have something to play with. If the classroom does not have enough store-bought materials, try having the children create their own learning materials. You can create a rich learning environment by bringing in cardboard boxes for construction or having the children help make homemade playdough.

Build on Children's Interests

To find materials that meet the needs of your classroom, use the guiding principle of emergent curriculum: follow the children's interests. Children remain more engaged in learning if the learning materials relate to subjects that they like.

 Case Study: Solving a Dinosaur Shortage

Many children in Winnie's classroom love dinosaurs. Winnie only has a few plastic dinosaurs for them to play with, so she decides to bring dinosaurs into the curriculum in other ways. To start, she places books about dinosaurs in the classroom library and reads them with the children during circle time and free-choice time. Winnie notices that even if she begins by reading to just one child, several more always come over to listen.

A few days later, Winnie brings in some cardboard boxes and suggests that the children build their own dinosaur using what they have learned. So many children want to participate that Winnie has to bring in more boxes the next day and split the children into several groups. By following the children's lead, she has created a learning-rich environment full of excited students.

Join In

The teacher can encourage children's curiosity by participating with them in classroom activities. When the teacher only observes the classroom, he may miss out on many key learning experiences. On the other hand, if he sits in different centers with the children and talks and plays with them, not only does he get to truly to observe their developing skills, but he also sends the message that the classroom activities are worthy of interest. Similarly, if a teacher wants the children to sing and dance during circle time, he must sing and dance too. Not only do the children learn the words and actions, but they also see their teacher having fun, which often increases their desire to participate.

Avoid Dwelling on Discipline

When a teacher spends the majority of his time chasing children around the room and telling them to stop certain behaviors, the entire class will not want to participate in activities. From their perspective, why try to do anything if someone will just tell them no?

To avoid disciplining children all day, start with proactive planning. If you select activities based on the children's interests, some negative behaviors automatically decrease—the children are so busy enjoying their learning that they do not have time to create problems. However, if a child begins showing a challenging behavior, you need to cut it off while preserving the child's motivation to learn. Try redirecting him to an area of the classroom that you know will engage him. Even better, find a positive model, whether a teacher or another child, to show the child how to participate appropriately in the activity.

 Case Study: Redirecting Superheroes

At the art center, teacher Zachary talks with Cadence about the paint colors she is mixing. In the middle of their conversation, Ubay and Pepita start chasing each other across the room. "Look out! Here comes Super Pepita!" Pepita shouts.

"You can't get me! I'm Ubay Man!" Ubay responds.

Zachary thinks fast about how to restore order before someone gets hurt. Remembering that both of these "superheroes" love painting, he says, "Super Pepita and Ubay Man, what colors are your hero capes?"

"Um . . . green!" says Pepita.

"Mine's purple!" says Ubay.

"Wow! Will you use your walking feet and come paint me a picture of them?" Zachary beckons, and the "superheroes" walk toward the art center. He smiles at Cadence and says, "You've mixed all sorts of colors today. Will you help me show Pepita and Ubay how to make the colors they need?"

"Okay," Cadence says.

Ways to Build Problem-Solving Skills

Asking and Answering Questions

To begin teaching children to problem solve, let them ask questions. In most preschool classrooms, this likely happens without any adult prompting. Children ask why the teacher has a red car, what he ate for breakfast, how he learned to read, and any other questions

they can think of. You might feel overwhelmed with how many questions you hear in a single day. However, one key to setting up a problem-solving classroom is to answer queries patiently. If children receive brusque or condescending responses, they will eventually stop asking questions, and while that might come as a relief to a busy teacher, it will also hinder children's future ability to learn. A classroom that encourages learning is a classroom that encourages questions. Try these tips for answering a child's questions:

- Keep answers at a developmentally appropriate level so that you do not overwhelm the child. Relate answers to topics and content that a child of that age can understand. For example, if four-year-old Molly asks, "When did you learn to read, Teacher?" you could say something like this: "Molly, I was only a little bit older than you when I learned to read. At first, my mother and my teacher read books to me. Then I started to remember some words, and finally, I was brave and started trying to read the words myself."
- Use mostly familiar vocabulary. If you introduce a new word, make sure to define it with vocabulary that the child already knows.
- If you do not know the answer to a question, it is okay to say so. If possible, model for the child how to find the answer.
- If a child asks an open-ended question that may not have one correct answer, ask the child to brainstorm what he thinks the answer is.

Children can learn a great deal by asking adults questions, but they can also learn when adults ask them questions. You can ask two basic kinds of questions: simple and open ended.

Many simple questions require only a one-word answer, often yes or no. They also frequently have only one correct answer. Simple questions often start with *what* or *when*, such as "What do you want for dinner?" While there could be many multiword answers to this question, they probably require little brainstorming. Teachers must ask simple questions throughout the day, such as to find out whether a child has washed his hands or would like a second helping at lunch. However, to encourage deeper thinking and build problem-solving skills, simple questions are not enough, as the following case study illustrates.

 Case Study: Simple Question Gone Wrong

Amelia, wearing an orange dress and pulling her mother, Opal, by the hand, skips into her classroom. Teacher Joaquin says, "You have such a bright dress on today, Amelia. What color is it?"

Amelia looks at the dress and proudly states, "Pink!"

"Oh," Joaquin says as he and Opal try not to laugh. Before either adult can say anything else, Amelia scampers off to the block center. "I guess we need to practice our colors today," Joaquin says with a wry smile. Opal chuckles.

Open-Ended Questions

An *open-ended question* from an adult requires a child to brainstorm, imagine, and articulate a response. Open-ended questions can have multiple correct answers. They often start with *how* or *why*, such as "How did the bear climb to the top of the mountain?" "Why did the tower fall down when you put the last block on top?" or "How do we build the bridge so that it won't fall down?" Responses to these types of questions frequently must include detailed explanations.

Teachers can also use *open-ended statements*, such as "I wonder why the bear sat on the wall" or "Tell me about what you did this weekend," to encourage a child to respond in detail. These types of prompts do not lead a child to a certain answer, so he can go anywhere with his response. Note that when using open-ended questions or statements, you need to be prepared to listen to the child's response. Even if it takes longer than you would like, this action helps the child feel that his answer matters and that you care.

When listening to a child's answer to an open-ended question, make sure to validate each response. Of course, some suggestions and answers may not be logical or feasible. Instead of immediately dismissing such a response, you can extend the child's learning by asking him how to make the idea happen. For example, if a child says that the class could build a ladder up to the sky to see what the clouds look like, you could ask what materials you would need to build a ladder that tall and how you could make sure that the ladder would not fall down. Though you will sometimes need to explain that not every idea will work out, even seemingly ridiculous proposals can help children develop their problem-solving skills.

Practicing Estimation

Estimation is an early math skill and a way for children to begin learning to form a *hypothesis*, or an educated guess based on research. To introduce the concept of estimation, try filling a clear jar with gumballs and asking the children to estimate, or guess, how many there are. Some children will say outlandish numbers for dramatic effect, so explain that the goal of the activity is to make an accurate guess, not to be silly. If the children do not know where to begin, offer an initial estimate as a model. Once everyone has guessed, add a hands-on component to the activity by opening the jar and counting the gumballs with the children. This will help them practice rote counting and give them an idea of what a realistic estimate is for this type of activity.

Many preschool classrooms use charts to start teaching estimation. For example, the teacher privately asks each child whether he prefers the color pink or the color blue. Then the teacher asks the entire class to guess how many children chose pink and how many chose blue. The children can estimate the total votes for each color, and then the teacher can make a graph to show what the true numbers are.

As with responses to open-ended questions or statements, do not penalize children for incorrect estimates. In fact, if you participate in the activity and accidently estimate incorrectly, it reinforces the fact that adults do not know everything and that it is okay to get an answer wrong. When children do not fear the consequences of guessing wrong, they are much more likely to offer estimates. They also will more likely participate if estimation becomes a regular part of classroom activities.

Teaching the Scientific Method

The *scientific method* is a way to collect information, make the best possible guess about how and why things happen, and test that guess. For many years, people tended to view the scientific method as a technique only for professional researchers. However, adults in all industries use the scientific method every day, often without realizing it, as they encounter problems, attempt to find the sources of those problems, and create possible solutions. For instance, a store manager may notice that sales have dropped at his store. As he talks to coworkers and customers and searches the internet for information about why this might be happening, he discovers that a competing store has opened down the street. The manager then creates a possible solution: he decides to temporarily lower prices at his store to get more customers to come in, see the quality of his products, and hopefully continue buying from his store.

As this example demonstrates, the scientific method is an important tool no matter what field a person works in. Therefore, teachers need to help children learn to use the scientific method as soon as the children have the cognitive capacity to do so. Although the term *scientific method* may sound highly technical, the process is simple and easy to use in an early childhood classroom.

Steps of the Scientific Method

1. Ask a question.
2. Collect information to help you answer the question.
3. Make a hypothesis about what the answer to your question might be.
4. Test your hypothesis.
5. Gather data from your test.
6. Make a conclusion—was your hypothesis correct or not?
7. Share your results and conclusion with your chosen audience.

What would these steps look like in the preschool classroom?

Case Study: Forrest's Block-Tower Experiment

1. **Ask a question:** Forrest asks, "How tall can I build my block tower before it falls down?"
2. **Collect information to help you answer the question:** Forrest asks his classmates how tall they have built towers before the towers collapsed, what types of blocks they used, and whether they built their towers on the floor or on tables.
3. **Make a hypothesis:** Forrest predicts that he can build a tower from the floor to the top of his shoulder using the classroom's large wooden blocks.
4. **Test your hypothesis:** Forest builds a tower with his chosen blocks. Each time he adds a block, he counts the total number of blocks to determine how tall the tower is. He continues to build until the tower falls down.
5. **Gather data from your test:** In his last count before the tower collapses, Forrest finds that he has fifteen blocks stacked on top of each other and that the resulting tower reaches from the floor to his collarbone.
6. **Make a conclusion:** Forrest concludes that he cannot build a tower up to the top of his shoulder with the large wooden blocks.
7. **Share your results:** During circle time, Forrest tells his friends how his experiment went and what he concluded.

Tips for Teaching the Scientific Method

To create a classroom where children use the scientific method, you need to understand your role in this process:

- Establish an environment in which children can ask questions. When they do, frequently respond, "Let's find out!"
- Instead of stepping in immediately to fix a problem, allow children to become slightly frustrated. If children can identify problems on their own, they will more likely want to fix those problems themselves.
- Provide a large amount of free-choice time in the daily schedule so that children can interact with classroom materials and brainstorm about different ways to use them.
- Prompt the children with open-ended questions or statements during free-choice time to help them ask questions that they can possibly find answers to.
- Allow children to test out hypotheses even if they seem flawed. Children should learn at a young age that not all educated guesses will be correct and that that is okay.
- Let children move through the scientific method at their own pace instead of stepping in to complete portions for them. It will take longer, but they will learn much more.

- Facilitate problem solving by occasionally creating small roadblocks for the children to overcome. Model how to overcome a roadblock, and then teach that process to the children. For example, if the children are creating a fort with sticks and a tarp on the playground, you could ask, "What would happen if the fort fell down on a windy day?" This question gives the children the opportunity to think about the possibilities while building the fort. If the children have trouble thinking of a solution, try narrating your thoughts as you describe how you might solve this problem: "If the fort fell down on a windy day, the tarp might blow away. How could I keep it from blowing away? Well, I could . . ."
- When children begin to brainstorm potential hypotheses, remind them that more than one answer can be correct and that they can test out multiple theories.
- Frequently ask children to help in the classroom, such as by setting the table before lunch or cleaning up an unexpected mess. To avoid resistance to these requests ("No! I want to play!"), make this assistance a regular part of the school day, such as by using a helper chart with jobs that rotate each week. Having responsibilities gives children a sense of empowerment. In turn, if children feel more empowered in the classroom, they may more readily offer hypotheses when brainstorming.
- For circle time or other reading times, choose books in which the characters resolve a problem. Ask the children simple questions during the story to help them identify what the characters are doing.

Because children are naturally creative, they can generate many questions and ways to answer them. Thus, the teacher's primary role in the scientific method is to help children feel comfortable confronting a question or problem and to remind them that they can try to find an answer on their own. A teacher's confidence in children may strongly contrast with what they learn about themselves at home. For example, when family members constantly tell a child not to touch things because he might break them, he begins to believe that he cannot do anything right, so he may hesitate to jump in and solve problems at school. In other families, adults try to prevent children from ever facing problems on their own. For example, a family might not expect their five-year-old to clean his own room or assist with any daily chores, even if he is developmentally capable of doing so. This method of child-rearing can lead the child to struggle with identifying problems and finding possible solutions. Because he lacks experience with both tasks, he may not believe that he can do either.

This is why play is such an essential part of the early childhood classroom. If children play with all materials and in all locations in the room, they will encounter problems. Two children will want to wear the same costume. Block towers will fall down. Paintings will get ruined. This is the nature of an exploratory environment. When a problem arises, the teacher needs to offer open-ended questions. Asking "What could we do to make sure everyone has a chance to wear the firefighter costume?" allows the child an opportunity to begin to formulate possible solutions. When he offers his ideas to the teacher, the teacher can encourage him to try out those possibilities and see what happens. This type of environment will help children become skilled thinkers and creators.

chapter 11

Using Process-Based Artwork to Enrich Emergent Curriculum

When you review a preschool lesson plan, you will always find a daily artwork component. Arts and crafts have become tangible daily products that show families what their preschoolers do over the course of the day. Unfortunately, most classroom art centers no longer promote creative art. Instead, they encourage children to reproduce projects that a teacher has previously assembled. The focus has changed to making bulletin-board-worthy end products instead of allowing children to truly enjoy creative expression.

What Is Art?

We often use the terms *arts* and *crafts* interchangeably, but they refer to two different types of projects. In a *craft*, participants use identical art supplies to construct their own copies of the same end product. In *art*, on the other hand, participants use different types of art supplies (for example, paint, chalk, crayons, and ink) to creatively express themselves. It does not matter what the end product looks like, as long as its creator enjoys the journey of making the art. In other words, making art involves process-based learning, and making crafts involves product-based learning. In an emergent-curriculum classroom, children should primarily make art rather than crafts.

Art (Process-Based Learning)	Crafts (Product-Based Learning)
• No step-by-step directions • Does not include a teacher-made sample for children to copy • Never has a right way or wrong way to complete it • Looks different for each student • Children not required to complete it in a specific way • Focuses on the materials the child uses (such as paint or chalk), the tools that shape the materials (such as a paintbrush or a stamp), and the experience of creating • Should be a pleasant experience for each child	• Has specific directions that must be followed in step-by-step order • Teacher must make a sample piece for children to copy • Has a right way and a wrong way to complete it • Can cause children to become frustrated if their work does not look identical to the teacher's • Looks almost exactly the same no matter which child completed it • Teacher may attempt to alter children's finished work to help all products look the same • Entire class participates • Ideas and directions often found on the internet

Encouraging Process-Based Art in the Classroom

Materials and Procedures for the Art Center

The teacher needs to look at how she has set up the art area and art activities in the classroom and ensure that they encourage process-based art instead of product-based crafts. First, children should have access to the art area throughout the day. Children need ample time to express themselves through their artwork, so the art center should be just as available to the children as all the other centers. So that the teacher does not have to constantly clean up the area, she should establish a routine at the beginning of the school year: If a child uses the materials in the art area, the same child cleans up the art area when she finishes.

The art area should include a variety of materials. Not only should children have daily access to crayons, markers, and pencils, but they should also have opportunities to interact with messy-art materials such as paint, chalk, and glue. These multisensory experiences enrich learning.

Even when the teacher has planned a certain art activity for the day, the children should always have access to an easel to paint or draw. The easel helps children work on the tripod grasp (because the angle of the surface makes it too difficult to use a palmar grasp), and it also allows them the creative freedom to paint or draw whatever ideas they choose.

Art centers should include a collage center. This area contains many loose parts with which the children can create. Of course, the collage center needs paper, scissors, tape, and glue for traditional two-dimensional collages, but it should also include a variety of open-ended materials, such as yarn, buttons, dried beans, beads, and so on that children can use to create three-dimensional artwork. All loose parts give children the chance to imagine something truly new and create it, but in particular, making collages with loose parts allows children to problem solve, imagine, reason, improve fine motor skills, and improve eye-hand coordination. Even if making collages creates a small mess in the classroom, the benefits far outweigh the inconvenience.

Safeguards for Messy Art

For children to take full advantage of a multisensory art center that encourages creativity, they need to be able to work without fear of getting paint, glue, or other substances on their clothes. Families or teachers need to provide smocks or art shirts so children do not become covered in their own artwork. Nonetheless, accidents can still happen, so teachers also need to explain to families why children need to wear play clothes to school each day instead of expensive clothes that cannot get dirty. If a child feels free to play without worrying about getting messy, she will more readily participate not only in art activities but also in other learning experiences that she might otherwise avoid, such as playing in a sand table. Families must understand that preschool is not a fashion show and that a quality preschool education includes getting dirty.

The Tools of Art

Along with having an always-open art area, teachers need to plan daily process-based art activities so the children can try new experiences. These lesson plans typically specify the art materials in use and the tools with which the artists manipulate those materials, but they do not state what the final products should look like. For example, the lesson plan may say that the children will create marble paintings. This type of art involves dipping marbles in paint and then rolling them around on paper. In this scenario, the art material is paint, and the tools are marbles. However, the lesson plan does not give any requirements for what the paintings should depict, what colors they should use, and so on—those details are up to the children, and no two paintings will look exactly the same.

Teachers can use many different tools to help create unique art experiences. The following list includes some of the most common choices:

- Children's own fingers (fingerpainting)
- Cotton balls
- Bubble cushioning wrap
- Matchbox cars
- Loofahs or other shower sponges
- Flyswatters
- Bubble wands (for blowing colored bubbles onto paper to make prints)
- Combs
- Kitchen brushes (such as basting brushes or cleaning brushes)
- Aluminum foil
- Feathers
- String
- Pipe cleaners
- Golf balls
- Cotton swabs

- Toilet plungers (new, unused ones only!)
- Toothbrushes
- Squirt bottles
- Straws (to blow paint through)
- Lego prints
- Magnets (put one magnet in paint on top of paper and use another magnet underneath to move first magnet)
- Roller brushes
- Outdoor materials, such as sticks and leaves
- Potato mashers

Along with using a variety of tools, the teacher can also plan a variety of locations or positions in which the children can create art. The following list includes some of the most common ideas:

- Painting or doing rubbings outdoors
- Painting while lying on one's back under a table, like Michelangelo painting the Sistine Chapel
- Painting or drawing while lying on one's stomach on a swing
- Painting while sitting inside a cardboard box

Teaching Process-Based Art

Because process-based art does not involve making an exact replica of a teacher's artwork, some children may not initially know how to begin. One of the best ways that the teacher can show them what to do is to sit down and participate with the art materials. Children learn by observation, so if they see their teacher experimenting with different tools, colors, or materials, it will encourage the children to do the same thing.

When the teacher introduces a new planned art lesson, she should demonstrate that activity during the opening circle time for that day. For example, if the lesson plan calls for the children to make prints with bubble cushioning wrap, the teacher brings the materials to the carpet and shows how to dip the wrap into the paint and press it to the paper. Note, though, that she should not require any child to complete an art activity exactly as demonstrated. For instance, it is perfectly acceptable for a child to choose to sit at the art table and use the bubble cushioning wrap like a paintbrush instead of making prints. The teacher simply shows one method of using the tool so that the children can begin the creative process themselves.

When a child completes an art activity, whether based on a planned lesson or her own ideas, she will often present the finished art to her teacher. The teacher may feel strongly tempted to say, "Beautiful" or "Awesome" or to specifically ask the child, "What is it?" Even though the teacher means well, these comments can deeply upset a child who has spent a long time preparing a piece. She is so proud of her work, and that is all the response she gets? Instead of giving generic praise or asking what the piece is, the teacher can begin with an open-ended statement to allow the child to describe her work, such as "Tell me about your picture," "What does your picture make you feel like?" or "What do you like best about your painting?" Each of these statements allows the child to provide information about the piece without feeling that the teacher is judging any of its aspects. These statements also invite the child to utilize her full vocabulary to attempt to describe what she has created.

When a child finishes a piece of artwork, the teacher can ask whether the child would like the teacher to include any words on the piece. Some children like to have the teacher write a title or a description of what they have drawn. Others simply want their names written on their artwork. If the child specifically tells the teacher not to write on the art, the teacher needs to respect that request. The child has worked diligently to create the piece, and she may feel that adding writing would ruin it. If the teacher still wants to put the child's name on the artwork to make sure that it eventually goes home with the right person, she can wait until any wet components (such as glue or paint) dry and then write the child's name in an inconspicuous spot, such as on the back or the bottom of the masterpiece.

Crafts and Coloring Sheets

Many teachers ask whether crafts have any place in the preschool classroom. Crafts should never be the primary focus of the art center, because the art center mostly relies on the learning tool of self-expression. Crafts, in contrast, use the learning tool of following directions, and the two tools often do not mesh well. However, crafts can occasionally appear in the art curriculum. They work well for occasional holiday gifts, such as the famous handprint turkey at Thanksgiving; expressions of thanks, such as for celebrating Mother's Day; or classroom decorations for a learning celebration, such as a party in honor of finishing a classroom project.

If the teacher does plan a craft activity, she should follow the same practice used in her other learning centers and not force any child to participate. The teacher can offer each child the opportunity, but she should respect the wishes of anyone who says no. If a child does participate in a craft, it is also perfectly acceptable for her to change the end product. Although the typical goal of a craft is to follow directions to construct a specific end product, if the child has another plan, the teacher should encourage that creativity.

Teachers also ask whether they can or should use coloring sheets in their art centers. These types of assignments specifically show children that there is only one correct way to complete a certain activity. If a child does not follow the directions laid out on the paper—such as if she colors outside the lines—then she has failed. The primary purpose of the art center is to allow children to express themselves, but coloring sheets restrict children instead. Because the entire purpose of the process-based classroom is to learn through experiences, not to create perfect products, these materials are not appropriate for this learning environment.

References and Recommended Reading

American Academy of Pediatrics. 2009. "Newborn Reflexes." American Academy of Pediatrics. https://www.healthychildren.org/English/ages-stages/baby/Pages/Newborn-Reflexes.aspx

American Academy of Pediatrics. 2019. "Developmental Milestones: 4-to-5-Year-Olds." American Academy of Pediatrics. https://healthychildren.org/English/ages-stages/preschool/Pages/Developmental-Milestones-4-to-5-Year-Olds.aspx

Bassok, Daphna, Scott Latham, and Anna Rorem. 2016. "Is Kindergarten the New First Grade?" *AERA Open* 2(1): n.p. https://doi.org/10.1177/2332858415616358

Berk, Laura. 2012. *Child Development*. 9th ed. London, UK: Pearson.

Center for Family Services. 2019. "School-Readiness Goals." Center for Family Services. https://www.centerffs.org/headstart/school-readiness-goals

Child Development Institute. n.d. "The Stages of Intellectual Development in Children and Teenagers." Child Development Institute. https://childdevelopmentinfo.com/child-development/piaget/#.XP_quNNKiys

Dodge, Diane Trister, Sherie Rudick, and Kai-Leé Berke. 2011. *The Creative Curriculum for Preschool*. 6th ed. Bethesda, MD: TeachingStrategies.

Ginsburg, Kenneth, the Committee on Communications, and the Committee on Psychosocial Aspects of Child and Family Health. 2007. "The Importance of Play in Promoting Healthy Child Development and Maintaining Strong Family Member–Child Bonds." *Pediatrics* 119(1): 182–191.

Harms, Thelma, Richard Clifford, and Debby Cryer. 2015. *Early Childhood Environment Rating Scale*. 3rd ed. New York, NY: Teachers College Press.

Kentucky Governor's Office of Early Childhood. n.d. "School Readiness in Kentucky." Kentucky Governor's Office of Early Childhood. https://kidsnow.ky.gov/families/readiness/Documents/school-readiness-definition.pdf

Miller, Susan, Ellen Booth Church, and Carla Poole. 2019. "Ages and Stages: Learning to Follow Directions." Scholastic. https://www.scholastic.com/teachers/articles/teaching-content/ages-stages-learning-follow-directions/

Montessori, Maria. 1948. *The Discovery of the Child*. Madras, India: Kalakshetra Press.

Montessorium. 2015. "Sandpaper Letters." Montessorium. https://montessorium.com/encyclopedia/sandpaper-letters

Parten, Mildred. 1932. "Social Participation among Preschool Children." *Journal of Abnormal and Social Psychology* 27(3): 243–269.

Piaget, Jean. 1952. *The Origins of Intelligence*. New York, NY: International Universities Press.

Pianta, Robert, Karen La Paro, and Bridget Hamre. 2008. *Pre-K–3 CLASS Manual*. Charlottesville, VA: Teachstone Training.

Reggio Children—International Center for the Defense and Promotion of the Rights and Potentials of All Children. n.d. "Atelier." Reggio Children—International Center for the Defense and Promotion of the Rights and Potentials of All Children. https://www.reggiochildren.it/activities/atelier/?lang=en

Sanders, Steve. 2015. *Encouraging Physical Activity in Toddlers*. Lewisville, NC: Gryphon House.

Searcy, Angela. 2019. *PUSH PAST It! A Positive Approach to Challenging Classroom Behaviors*. Lewisville, NC: Gryphon House.

TeachingStrategies. 2010. *TeachingStrategies GOLD: Objectives for Development and Learning: Birth through Kindergarten*. Washington, DC: TeachingStrategies.

Welch, Ginger. 2019. *How Can I Help? A Teacher's Guide to Early Childhood Behavioral Health*. Lewisville, NC: Gryphon House.

Women's Bureau of the US Department of Labor. 1999. "The Women's Bureau, What It Is, What It Does." Women's Bureau of the US Department of Labor. https://archive.mith.umd.edu/womensstudies/GenderIssues/WomenInWorkforce/womens-bureau.html

Index